Money
Still Doesn't
Grow on Trees

Money Still Doesn't Grow on Trees

A PARENT'S GUIDE TO RAISING
FINANCIALLY RESPONSIBLE
TEENAGERS AND YOUNG ADULTS

Neale S. Godfrey

WITH TAD RICHARDS

RODALE

© 2004 by Neale Godfrey

Interior illustrations © 2004 by Tad Richards

All rights reserved. No part of this publication may be reproduced or transmitted in any form or by any means, electronic or mechanical, including photocopying, recording, or any other information storage and retrieval system, without the written permission of the publisher.

Printed in the United States of America
Rodale Inc. makes every effort to use acid-free ⊗, recycled paper ♻.

Interior illustrations by Tad Richards

Book design by Leanne Coppola/Abbate Design

Library of Congress Cataloging-in-Publication Data

Godfrey, Neale S.
    Money still doesn't grow on trees : a parent's guide to raising
financially responsible teenagers and young adults / Neale S. Godfrey
with Tad Richards.
       p.   cm.
    Includes index.
    ISBN 1–57954–851–2 paperback
    1. Teenagers—Finance, Personal. 2. Young adults—Finance, Personal.
3. Finance, Personal. 4. Parenting. I. Richards, Tad. II. Title.
HG179 .G632 2004
332.024'00835   2003019144

Distributed to the book trade by St. Martin's Press

2 4 6 8 10 9 7 5 3 1 paperback

RODALE

WE **INSPIRE** AND **ENABLE** PEOPLE TO IMPROVE
THEIR LIVES AND THE WORLD AROUND THEM

FOR MORE OF OUR PRODUCTS
WWW.RODALESTORE.COM
(800) 848-4735

To Georgine Axelrod (1922–2003)

To my mother, always the best role model for my sisters and me, whom you raised to be strong women. This is in memory of the loving poems you always wrote us and the crossword puzzles you were never without.

This particular crossword puzzle certainly doesn't come close to your standards for rhyme or sophistication, but it's done with great creativity, so that for the first time the answers go not only across and down, but backward and bottom up. And they meet your most important standard . . . they're done with love.

I love you, Mommy, and you're always with Malla, Alison, and me. I know that you will always look down on us and remember the good times behind all these words.

Dedication Crossword Puzzle

ACROSS

1. You traveled with Lysol to disinfect the tub,
   To pick a hotel without one was a great big flub.

5. During the holiday season you were always there,
   Personnel manager extraordinaire!

11. Every Sunday you'd make all those tiny words fit,
    You're the only person who could always complete it.

12. Thespians, costumes, actors galore,
    Old musicals, yes, and new plays to explore.

14. To some he might seem like an English snob,
    But to you, he was your handsome actor heartthrob.

15. Police never gave her a ticket because she treated them with respect.
    (In Ady's old Lincoln, Alison threw up down her neck.)

BACKWARD

16. In public you never, ever copped an attitude.
    This was your favorite color—never, ever your mood.

DOWN

2. Your favorite form of relaxation,
   That toasty, roasty, tanning sensation.

3. Building our character, to the beach we go;
   At the governor's picnic, our attire quite the show.

4. Your mom—always schlepping a shopping bag
   (Jars of chicken soup and matzoh balls would make it sag).

6. Your warmth, your comfort, your support in every folly,
   Your confidante, your love . . . your Grandma Molly.
   (Sorry, Mommy—I know you're not supposed to put the word in the
   definition, but . . .)

7. Your favorite pastime, at which you were the master,
   Always shaking your head that your three schnooks couldn't do it faster.

9. A dancer with Martha Graham, one joy you'd always give—
   The motto that defined you: "To dance is to live."

12. Whenever we kids were grumpy and sad,
    You'd do your hoofing to make us glad.

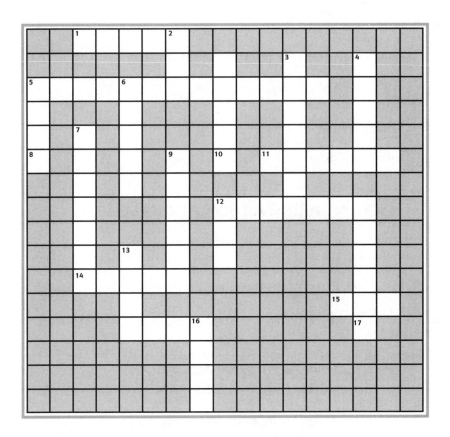

13. On a special snow excursion you got dumped off his sled.
    He's always been in your heart and in your head.

16. He taught you "back-to-basics": work, pay cash, own your own house.
    He was kind, solid, quick as a fox but quiet as a mouse.

UP

8. Your loving husband with whom you'd dance and swing,
   Also known as New Jersey's cottage cheese king.

10. You could spell all of them and even have fun,
    And didn't mind when we'd call you for the definition of one.

17. Long talks and cream cheese we never could miss,
    Who knew creepy little fish eggs could taste like this?

(Please turn to page x for puzzle answer.)

CONTENTS

Puzzle Answer

To Dedication Crossword on page vi

		¹B	A	T	H	²S									
						U		S			³B			⁴J	
⁵B	L	O	O	⁶M	I	N	G	D	A	L	E	S		E	
R				O				R			R			W	
E		⁷R		L				O			M			E	
⁸H		E		L		⁹B		¹⁰W		¹¹P	U	Z	Z	L	E
		A		Y		A				D				
		D				L		¹²T	H	E	A	T	E	R	
		I				L		A						A	
		N		¹³J		E		P						I	
		¹⁴G	R	A	N	T								V	
				K									¹⁵C	A	R
				E	U	L	¹⁶B						¹⁷C		
							I								
							L								
							L								

Has a mutant teenage alien invaded your house?

Introduction

WHY EVERY PARENT OF A TEENAGER NEEDS THIS BOOK

Is it too late to create a financially functional home when your kids are teenagers? Is it impossible to start with a teenager and create a financially responsible human being?

Sometimes it sure seems that way.

In the very early days of working on this book, I went out to the Chester Diner for a late snack, and a wonderful teenage boy named Jeff was my waiter. I had a notebook with me, and he asked if I was a writer. I told him yes, I was working on a book about how to teach financial responsibility to teenagers. I asked if he had any advice.

"Yes," he said. "It's very simple. If your parents do everything for you—like if they buy you a car and pay for the insurance—you're screwed."

If you're like the parents that Jeff talked about, and you've come late to the idea of developing financially responsible kids, this task can seem like squeezing toothpaste back into the tube. And even if you're not—and you've been following the advice in my earlier books, *Money Doesn't Grow on Trees* and *A Penny Saved;* you've created a Work-for-Pay allowance plan and a Jar System for saving and spending; and you've played Want versus Need games, confident that your kids have the most solid grounding since the discovery of stain-proof indoor-outdoor carpeting—you can still wake up one morning and find that a stranger, an alien being from a different planet, has moved into your house.

Or perhaps it's a mutant alien being from two different planets. Sometimes the stranger seems to be from the planet INEED, as in "I need designer clothes. I need to be entertained. I need what everyone else has." And it's equally likely that the teenage alien is from the planet IWONT, as in "I won't clean my room. I won't wear the clothes you pick out for me. I won't come in on time. I won't do nuttin."

So, whether all of this is new to you or you've been working right along, teaching your kids money skills and values, there will be times when you'll want to throw your hands up in despair.

But, of course, you can't. None of us can. We're parents, and that means we keep trying, and we cling to the faith that against all odds, we'll get through to our kids with the message that this is Planet Earth and that's the planet they have to live on.

This is particularly important when it comes to money issues, because they can bite back with such a vengeance, and so quickly.

- According to a recent study by Harvard law professor Elizabeth Warren, 120,000 young people between the ages of 18 and 25 declared bankruptcy in 2001. This number has increased by 51 percent in the past 10 years—and these juvenile financial delinquents account for more than 7 percent of all bankruptcies.

- More people in the United States declare bankruptcy than graduate from college.

- The average college student owed $2,748 in credit card debt in 2000, and that represented a 67 percent increase—not over a decade but in 2 years.

- Almost 60 percent of young adults have carried up to $25,000 of consumer debt.

- Because of their financial decisions, 24 percent of young adults have had to move back in with their parents.

- Almost 40 percent of young adults have saved only $5,000 or less.

It's not okay what society is doing to teenagers—preying on their financial naïveté with everything from deceptive advertising to the promise of easy credit.

It's not okay what teenagers are doing to themselves when they spin out into the orbits of INEED and IWONT.

And it's not okay if we let them stay ignorant. Teachers have to do their part, financial institutions have to do their part, but first and foremost, we as parents have to take responsibility for our teenagers' financial illiteracy.

Teenagers still live under our roofs, and we're still responsible for them. They look sort of like those little kids we remember from a few years ago—but they're different.

- The amount of money involved in teenagers' lives is greater than when they were younger. They can earn more, spend more, and get into debt. And even without the introduction of problems, their basic maintenance levels are higher.

- The amount of trouble they can get into is worse. It can have wider repercussions, and it can cost . . . oh, a lot more.

- Their bad habits are more deeply ingrained and harder to break.

The more time we spend working with our kids on money issues, the more we can prepare them to avoid some of these problems and deal with others.

If you've been teaching your kids about financial responsibility all along, only to see the wisdom you've imparted suddenly disappear into the ozone, those early lessons haven't gone away. They're just hiding, and they'll resurface—especially if you can shift gears now and learn to deal with the special problems of teenagers and money.

Hidden Lessons

Teaching money lessons to your kids is just like any other form of parent-child communication—it's always happening, whether you know it or not, whether you plan it or not.

According to a recent survey of 12- to 17-year-olds by the GE Center for Financial Learning in Richmond, Virginia:

- 71 percent of kids say they learn about money from their parents.

- 47 percent of kids, however, say their parents seldom or never discuss the issue.

Teens and Saving

Sixty-two percent of teens say they get most of their money from part-time employment, summer jobs, or neighborhood jobs such as babysitting or raking leaves. Over half (55 percent) say they work mainly for spending money. Another 35 percent mainly save the money they make.

Saving money is important to American teens; about nine out of 10 save money, though 36 percent admit that they're saving for specific items that they want to purchase. Almost one-quarter (22 percent) are saving for college, and 27 percent save for no particular reason. Four out of 10 say they save half or more of their money, and three out of four have a savings account.

Source: National Consumers League survey, 2002

If this is new to you, it's never too late to learn, and it's never too late to start. Teenagers listen more than we think they do. And even though they may act like aliens from one moment to another, they really do want to live on Planet Earth. In fact, despite the financial problems that many teens run into, some do "get it."

So no matter where your teenagers or young adults are with their financial common sense, we can all work at raising our kids' consciousness to a new level of financial responsibility.

In this book, I'll take you through three steps to creating more financially responsible teens.

First, we'll take a look at ourselves to see what messages we're sending to our kids. As kids grow to be teenagers, their observations of their parents' weak spots become more and more acute.

They sense our uncertainties, our conflicts, even our hypocrisies, and they'll use them. In order to develop good financial habits in our kids, we have to make sure we aren't enabling their bad habits.

In other words, if there's a problem in your kids' financial dynamic, then there's a problem in the family's financial dynamic, and everyone will need to work at changing it.

This does not—I repeat, *not*—mean that it's all your fault. Placing the whole load of responsibility on yourself is a barrier to solving the problem, just as much as shirking responsibility. "Whatever you do, you're wrong," a friend of mine used to say about parenting. I understood how she felt, but it's more useful to realize that we're right most of the time, yet we still have to make some adjustments.

If your kids are being irresponsible financially, it is their responsibility. They have to answer for debts they've accumulated, resources they've wasted, ways that they have been less-than-full citizens of the household. But recognizing irresponsibility, turning it around . . . these things don't just happen. Money doesn't grow on trees, and neither does wisdom.

Second, we'll identify negative trends that can develop with teenagers and money—and learn how to stop them. Lack of information and misinformation are the sources of almost all negative trends in teenage behavior, and they can be hard to overcome, especially since teenagers can be devastatingly literal about information when they choose to be. Like the day that my daughter, Kyle, then 13, decided to cut a large piece of cheese with a very large knife, while balancing the cheese on her thigh. In the emergency room, she glared at me accusingly and said:

"You never told me not to cut cheese on my thigh!"

Misinformation can be even worse, because kids get it from other kids, and so they have a tendency to cling to it like gospel, with potentially spiraling results.

Third, I'll guide you in developing positive attitudes for your teenagers and their money—and show you and your children proven methods to build strong habits that will last a lifetime. Young people need to learn the value of money, and they need to learn how to incorporate money into an overall philosophy of social, personal, and ethical values. This is, ultimately, what I write about and try to teach. Money is a tool. The more we learn to understand it and use it correctly, the more it becomes a positive force in a system of values. And that understanding, more than anything, is what our teenagers need to learn from us.

The great thing about money is . . . it's only money. It's not love or nurturing or memories—or any of those intangibles that can't be quantified. You can count it; you can measure it; you can budget it. This makes it a perfect vehicle for explaining responsibility and for explaining how the world works.

Money is a tool, a finite resource. You can allocate the same dollar to hot dogs or a Van Gogh poster, an Eminem CD or a computer . . . but not both. You can buy drugs with it, or you can donate it to help find a cure for breast cancer.

Yes, money can't buy happiness. But learning to use money responsibly can earn you self-esteem, and that's a large component of happiness.

Real families will show us how—and why—these three steps are so important. Throughout the book, you'll find case histories of everyday families whom I've worked with. You'll meet Amy, Kay, and other parents who have struggled, sometimes successfully, sometimes in deep water, with responsibility issues involving teenagers and money.

Amy is a particularly fascinating example. She's a nurse and a divorced mother of two teenage girls who have never developed a sense of responsibility about money—and as a result, Amy now finds herself panicky, depressed, and desperate. I've been working closely with Amy to turn her situation around, and the book will include a detailed account of our work together. Amy is all too representative of a great many families—single- or two-parent—who suddenly have to confront teenagers who have been "shielded" from money responsibilities for too long.

Amy and the families I've talked to in this book were in varying degrees of crisis or success with teenagers. What have they done right? What have they done wrong? What have they changed? What do they need to change? You may see yourself in one or more of them, maybe in stories in which the situation seems hopeless. But there's always hope.

Every situation can be turned around. And, yes, you *can* raise financially responsible teenagers and young adults in today's financially irresponsible world. So long as you and your child both understand that money *still* doesn't grow on trees.

PART 1

Taking a Look at Ourselves

1

WHERE DO KIDS GET THOSE IDEAS?

There's an interesting phenomenon that happens right about the same time that our children turn into monsters from outer space: We're turning into some kind of different creatures, too, often creatures that we don't approve of all that much.

You know the person I mean. The mom that we smirked at in Kmart when we were teenagers—the one who was there to buy lightbulbs and drapes, but somehow or other kept adding Barbie accessories and monster squirt guns and giant boxes of Popsicles to her shopping cart as her kids kept goading for more.

And you know the kids I mean. The ones who know exactly what they're doing.

The Nagging Factor

Number of times kids say that they have to nag a parent before she'll give in and buy them what they want: nine.

And face it . . . kids in Kmart have nothing better to do with their time. If we let them, they'll nag the nine times, or 10, or 11, until we give in. And if we let them nag nine times without putting a stop to it as soon as it starts, we will give in eventually. But think about it. Having someone beg you for something nine times doesn't make it suddenly become a good idea, does it? How does this sound?

"Gee, Mom, I'd really like some drugs. Can you buy them for me?"

Are you going to give in, even if they ask you nine times?

No, of course not. Why not? If you did, it would make your kid happy . . . in the short run. That's what drugs do—they make people happy in the short run. But we know that the destructiveness far outweighs that short-term pleasure.

It's the same thing with other material items. Not as awful, but the same thing. Giving something to a kid because he nags, begs, or wheedles is pleasurable in the short run to the kid—and to you, if you hear "I love you, Mom"—but in the long run it teaches a lesson that you don't want to teach.

Giving in is all about guilt. We give in to our kids, and later to our teenagers, because we feel guilty for one reason or another, and pretty soon we've become people we don't much like being.

What's the guilt about? Why the pressure? It comes from somewhere. So if the first step in the process of turning our kids around is to turn ourselves around, then the first step in turning ourselves around is to look in the mirror.

Although it sometimes feels as if parents have always felt guilty about not giving their kids enough, this is really a relatively new phenomenon. You didn't find starchy Victorian parents agonizing about whether they were giving their kids enough. Children were expected to know their place, to be seen and not heard. Depression-era parents may have agonized because there wasn't enough, but that wasn't about guilt—the kind of guilt that makes you want to overcompensate as you try to make it up to your kids for real or imagined shortcomings.

It's different now. We tend to have kids later in life, which means that when they're growing up, we're more advanced in our careers and more affluent.

Seventy percent of women work outside of the home these days, and you'd think that would be an established fact of life by now . . . but somehow, it isn't. We still get attacked for it, and we still feel guilty about it.

Guilt is a legitimate emotion in our day and age. Things are tough, and our problems are real. Conflicting demands on our time are real. Divorce is real—and the resulting pulls of two separate households. Your ex may well be indulging the kids in ways that you can't, especially if his income is higher and his face time with them is less. Even intact families are going to feel the pull of guilt. Time is at a premium, and we never seem to be able to apportion it right. Our kids have friends whose parents get them things we won't get for our kids, or let them do things we won't let our kids do . . . or at least, that's what we're told.

All you can do is hold on to your own values and stick to the rules that uphold those values. Remember that it's never going to be fair. The grass will always be greener in the next pasture. And all the other kids will always be allowed to do something or other, or get something or other.

An Alternate Take on Guilt

My sister Alison called me one day with the bubbly excitement of someone who's just discovered that the Tooth Fairy is real after all.

"You'll never guess what the kids' psychologist told me," my sister said.

"What?"

"I'm not using enough guilt."

"Don't be silly. You're a Jewish mother. Of course you're using enough guilt. And anyway, guilt is bad. We've been told that all our adult lives."

"It turns out we were told wrong. He told me I need to start honing my guilt skills."

When she explained it to me further, I realized it made a lot of sense. And I checked it out with a psychologist friend, who gave it a thumbs-up. Kids aren't always going to respond to reason. They like arguing too much. Given a chance, they'll slip into debate mode; then suddenly the whole objective becomes winning debate points, not having the reasonable discussion you were expecting. But the same kid who simply cannot be convinced that it's a good idea—and necessary for his own well-being—that he be home by 11 o'clock will come home at 11 o'clock, without thinking twice about it, if you can make him feel guilty enough for not doing it.

Their having a certain amount of guilt, he said, shows you that your kids have a conscience. This is a child-rearing technique that would not have worked on little Hannibal Lecter.

He tossed another distinction at me: good guilt versus bad guilt. And the difference is in what you use it for. Good guilt gets your kids to come in at 11. Bad guilt convinces them that they're bad human beings if they forget your birthday.

The Come-Clean-with-Yourself Quiz

To see if you're sending your kids the wrong messages about money, read the following questions and respond with either yes or no.

1. If your teenager asks for money, do you fork it over? Do you give money in response to nagging or wheedling or to— harder yet, because teenagers are more sophisticated at the psychology of wheedling—"I love you. . . . Can I have some money?"
   Yes _____   No _____

2. Are you afraid to say, "This doesn't fit into our budget"?
   Yes _____   No _____

3. Do you feel that your teens must have what other teens have?
   Yes _____   No _____

4. Do you make sure that your teenage kids are out of the room when you sit down to work on the family budget?
   Yes _____   No _____

5. Do you not let your kids look at the check when you go out to a restaurant?
   Yes _____   No _____

6. Do you use credit cards to buy stuff for your teenage kids when you know you shouldn't?
   Yes _____   No _____

7. Have you ever spent money on your teenage kids and not let your spouse know?
   Yes _____   No _____

8. Have you ever bought something for your teens because you didn't want your ex to be the one who got it for them?
   Yes _____   No _____

9. Do you use a shopping trip as a reward for good behavior?
   Yes ____ **No** ____

10. Do you know what your kids spend their own money on?
    Yes ____ **No** ____

If you answered yes (or no, to the last question) to more than eight of these, it means . . . Well, if you answered yes to more than seven, it means . . . Well, more than six . . . more than five . . .

Let's make it easy. If you answered yes to even one of these, it means that you're sending messages to your kids that you don't want to be sending.

One Wrong Answer Is a Failing Grade?

Tough test, eh? But it's okay. . . . I grade on a curve, and a score of one doesn't mean that you flunk out of parent class. We all do these things; we all probably fall into several of these categories. We're good parents striving to be better parents.

Do you give in when your teenager asks for money? It's hard not to. There is simply nothing more gratifying than putting a smile on the faces of those we love most in the world, of being able to make them happy.

But this is money—it's not magic. And it's not more special or valuable than a smile on your teenager's face or that hug that makes your knees go weak and leaves you walking around for the next hour with a goofy smile on your own face, until you notice that you're humming the same song that you yelled at her to turn down on the stereo.

And money is quantifiable—it's finite. You have a certain amount, and it has to be apportioned in a way that balances emotional well-being and the realities of dealing with a finite resource. Of course, you don't forget about the emotional well-being—not that any of us ever could.

AMY

"I DON'T KNOW HOW TO CHANGE."

Amy is a nurse and a divorced mother of two teenage girls who's found herself in over her head.

"I know I do it. Yep, I'm the original Yes-Mommy. Actually, I was tougher at one point in my life. But I hated it.

"There were times when we were really broke. The kids were little, I was working, and my husband Jake decided to quit his job and go to a culinary school. So we had only the one income, and of course the kids would go shopping with me, and I had to say 'not today' so many times. Then when Jake would take them out, they'd often come home with stuff we really couldn't afford.

"The answer they give in books is that you have to sit down with your spouse and agree that you're going to present a united front—but in real life that doesn't necessarily happen. I had those conversations with Jake all the time, and he would always agree. Then as soon as the conversation was over, he ignored it.

"Now I've been on my own for 3 years, and all the financial decisions are my own. But I still can't resist helping. The car payments, the new carburetor. Joanie's graduated from high school now, and she works, but she doesn't make enough to get by. And sometimes I do feel used. I know Joanie loves me, and we have a good relationship in so many ways, but the truth is that every time I hear 'I love you,' I'm waiting for the other shoe to drop.

"I don't know how to change. I don't think I can just quit cold turkey and tell her, 'Honey, from here on, you're on your own.' Is there another way to break the pattern?"

Amy's right to be concerned. Behavior doesn't change overnight.

If you have teens who haven't learned to handle money responsibly, that's a project. If they've gotten used to depending on you, they may not be able to handle suddenly being cut off. That's one of the main reasons that 120,000 people between the ages of 18 and 25 declare bankruptcy each year.

But think about it. How have you and your teenager handled it when it's been time to take on other large, adult responsibilities? How about driving a car? You didn't just hand your teen the keys one day and say, "Here you go. You're on your own." You took him out for lessons. You explained to him that a car is a huge, powerful, potentially lethal machine with no mind of its own, that he'll have to be responsible for everything that it does: starting, moving backward, moving forward, turning, stopping—even standing still after it's parked. He'll have to be responsible for turning on the lights when it's dark and using the signal lights when he wants to turn. He'll have to know where all the other cars on the highway are and develop an instinct for what they're going to do.

It's a lot to learn and a huge responsibility, and the idea that he's going to take it on is terrifying—generally more terrifying to you than to him, partly because you understand it all and he doesn't. So you introduce it to him gradually, one lesson at a time.

And when he has all that down, there's more. He has to remember to read the gas gauge and make sure the car doesn't run out of gas. He has to know how to put gas in the tank, and he has to have the money to pay for it. He has to know what the other gauges on the dashboard mean and what to do if they indicate trouble. He has to keep track of how long it's been since the oil was changed.

And there's still more. He has to take a test and get a driver's license. He has to get insurance.

And there's more than that. You teach defensive driving, and you teach that there's always a chance that something can go wrong. There could be an accident, so you make certain that your teen knows what do in case he's in one—who to call, how to report it, how to handle the situation responsibly—and never to leave the scene of an accident.

That's a lot of information, but it's all important. So you help him take it step by step, because all of it is stuff he's never done before, and he couldn't do it without you. But ultimately he'll learn, and he'll be able to do it on his own, and he'll be that much more grown-up.

It's the same thing with achieving financial independence and learning financial responsibility. Your children are not born knowing how to do it. They have to learn, which means you have to teach them—from the earliest lessons right down to how to deal with serious financial problems. I'll get to all of that, step by step, in the next section of this book.

But first, we have to look at ourselves.

This means giving up some of the old rules and making up some new rules.

Don't forget the example of "Mom, can I have some money for drugs?" Of course your teen isn't going to ask that. But it's a graphic example of the fact that we can draw a line, we can do it without even thinking twice, we know exactly why we're drawing it, and we have no problem drawing it. We aren't focusing on *Gee, I want to make my kid happy* or *What the heck—it'll buy me some peace and quiet.* We're going straight to *This isn't right for him.* And from there, it's an easy step to "No."

2

THE ONE PHRASE TO REMEMBER: "THIS DOESN'T FIT INTO OUR BUDGET"

Notice the wording here. "This doesn't fit into our budget" is not the same as "We can't afford it." If you can remember only one phrase from this entire book, this is the one—and use it often. The problem with "We can't afford it" is that it doesn't mean anything. In fact, you probably can afford it. If you were to go without eating for a week, you could afford to rent the limo to take the kids to the eighth-grade prom. If you took out a second mortgage on the house, you could build an inground pool in your backyard.

KAY

What She Really Wanted

Sometimes it's amazing how differently parents and kids see the same set of circumstances. Often when I work with families, I get striking examples of these different perspectives. Kay, 42, works in the registrar's office of a Midwestern state university; her husband is on the town's police force. They have a son in college, a daughter, Erina, just about to graduate from high school, and a son in junior high. They get by, and they're providing for their kids' education, but there's not a lot extra.

"That's why I made sure Erina had the prom dress she really wanted," Kay told me. "It wasn't in our budget, but I made room for it. I put it on layaway at the beginning of the school year, and I went without lunches for 6 *months* to pay for it. But it was worth it when I saw the way she glowed as she came down the stairs to meet her date on prom night."

I could see the love in her eyes as she recalled the night, and I could hear the pride in her voice at the sacrifice she'd made to give Erina her heart's desire.

And at the same time, I couldn't help wondering how Erina felt about it.

In the 1937 classic tearjerker *Stella Dallas,* Stella sacrifices everything she has so that her daughter, Laurel, can marry a rich and socially prominent young man.

And today, we're still suckers for maternal sacrifice. We get to see ourselves as the star of our own movie, but we always cast ourselves as Stella. No one ever actually fantasizes herself into the role of Laurel. In fact, the whole premise of the movie rests on Laurel's supreme ignorance of the entire drama. What if she knew that Mom was standing outside in the cold, with her nose pressed against the window?

What, indeed? I asked Erina about the dress, and she had two different responses, neither of which fit too neatly into a fantasy drama.

First response: "Oh, yeah, it was really nice. It wasn't exactly the style I would have picked out for myself, but it didn't show too much cleavage in the prom pictures, so I guess that made Mom happy—and you have to wear something, don't you? (She giggles.) I spilled some Pepsi on it. Well, I told Mom it was Pepsi. I guess that was kind of careless. But after all, when am I ever likely to wear it again?"

Second response, after I told her about the 6 months of lunches: tears. "I never wanted her to do *that*!!!"

So, it's okay to choose not to go without lunch for the prom gown. "It's not in our budget" is an acknowledgment of that choice. More than that, it means facing up to a truth that's hard to even think about.

My money, my choices.

The Budget Hierarchy

You not only have a right, you have a responsibility to set up a hierarchy in your budgeting. You have a right to a different life than your kids. You don't have to be Stella Dallas, and if the truth be known, your kids don't want you to either.

In some ways, that's obvious. You can drink legally; your kids can't. You can vote, and your under-18 kids can't. You can drive, and your underage children can't.

You get to pay less for car insurance than your kids, you can enter into legally binding contracts, and you can get a mortgage to buy a house.

In other words, all things being equal, all things aren't equal.

Let's stop here for a second and digest that, because it's a truth many of us have a hard time acknowledging.

But think about it. Your teenager may *need* Steve Madden shoes or a Fubu warmup jacket, but if you're working in an office that demands a certain standard of dress, you need a Donna Karan suit. There's a big difference between *need* and need. You don't have to buy the Steve Maddens just because you bought the Donna Karan.

Your kids can have input into the budget—and they should—and I'll spend some serious time talking about that later. But ultimately it's your job. You do have to be the one who says no.

My money, my choices. It's even hard to say.

"It's not my money," Kay told me, her expression intractable. "I could never be that selfish. It's my family's money."

Of course it is. We work for our families—we want to, we expect to. But when it comes to what happens to the bucks . . . the buck stops here. You're the family's CEO. You need to make the decisions about allocating resources.

A large expense like this is also a lesson in empowerment. You need to empower your teen to have control over her large spending decisions—both the decision making and the financing. Kay didn't tell Erina that she'd have to pay for part—or all—of the dress, and she didn't ask her what it was worth to her, what percentage of her finite resources she wanted to allocate to a prom dress. If you're not allocating any of your own resources—and you don't know what someone else is sacrificing for you—the sky can be the limit.

What's more, it's very important that your children—younger children and teens alike—understand that money is a personal possession. They know that their money is their own, and you reinforce that by respecting it. You don't steal from them; you don't "borrow" from them.

You need to reinforce this awareness when it comes to your money, too. Make sure they understand that it's not just one big communal chowder that anyone can dip into anytime they want. If you don't do that, you're giving them tacit permission to steal from you if they decide they need money for something.

Why else are we uncomfortable with saying around kids, "It doesn't fit into the budget"? Many of us grew up in families where money was tight, and we want to give our kids more than we had. But let's remember that we're responsible for giving our kids more than money, more than material things.

Kids need to have limits set. They need a sense of perspective, and they need to relate money to values.

We teach our kids values because they'll need them to conduct their lives when they move out on their own and the only parents to guide them will be the ones inside them. So we can't go on being magic mommies forever, pretending there are no limits. We need imposed limits, the product of intelligent decisions. Not "We can't afford it," but "It's not in our budget."

Taking this approach to your money choices is the critical first step toward teaching your kids about smart decision making with their money.

Now we have to take a closer look at some of the other messages we're sending our kids, and pay special attention to the mistakes that we may be making without even realizing it. Remember, those kids are watching your every move.

3

THE BIG MISTAKES

As parents, we all want our sons and daughters to grow up to be well-adjusted, responsible adults who look back on their childhoods—and on us, as their moms and dads—with fondness. None of us want our kids to be teased at school for their generic-brand sneakers or to have to worry about our increasing credit card debt or how we're going to make the monthly mortgage payment. But sometimes, in our quest to give our kids happy childhoods, we send the wrong messages about money—messages that can confuse our kids and harm the family's financial health.

Here are some of the most common mistakes parents make, and how you can avoid them.

Big Mistake #1: Believing That Your Kids Must Have What Other Kids Have

This is a pretty easy temptation to fall into. It probably goes back to our own childhoods. If we grew up having less than other kids, or feeling that we did, then we don't want it to happen to our children. That's a large part of why we worked so hard to succeed.

But the answer to it is easy, too.

Is this a value we want our children to have? Do we want them to have that sense of entitlement: "I should have what he has". . . "I gotta keep up with the Joneses." Of course we don't.

I'm not saying that your kids can't have anything; I'm talking about balance.

Okay, it's tough on a kid to be the only one in school who's wearing JC Penney sneakers instead of Air Jordans, and it's hard not to want to do something about that. But it's also tough to be the only kid with only one pair of Air Jordans when everyone else has a pair for every day of the week, and it's tough to be the only one driving a used Toyota when everyone else has a new Lexus.

And that, in a nutshell, is the main problem with keeping up with the Joneses. There's no cutoff point. Once you're in that mindset, nothing is ever enough. If the guy next door has a $150 Palm Pilot, and you can't imagine being without one, then you won't be able to imagine being without a $500 BlackBerry—or a $1,000 BlackBerry with special antennas.

It's not attractive. It's not what we want for ourselves, and it's certainly not what we want for our kids.

The solution: Stop and think. Why am I considering buying this for my kids? Will it help them do better in school? Will it add to their cultural enrichment? Will it help them develop skills that they need?

Or will it jack up their snob-appeal quotient?

There's nothing wrong with having nice things. But when kids get things without realizing the amount of money they cost—and, therefore, the number of hours worked to earn them—there is a value disconnect that can start a cycle of wanting, and getting, more and more without ever really being satisfied. When this happens, having nice things comes at a price that gets calculated in a different ledger, and it's a high price.

RON AND MARGE

The Most Out-of-Control Family I've Ever Worked With

I vividly remember the most out-of-control family that I've ever worked with. I was introduced to Ron and Marge on *Oprah* as a family who simply had no concept of limits for their kids. None. They could not imagine the possibility of not getting anything the kids said that they wanted.

The kids needed a room, then two rooms, for all the stuff they had. The parents were just barely scraping by for necessities on an annual income of

---

Shop Till You Drop

What do most people spend on holiday shopping? Here's a breakdown by income.

Under $30,000: $379

$30,000–$74,000: $618

$75,000 and over: $956

Source: *USA Today*

$35,000 between the two of them, but they spent $2,500 a year on Christmas for the kids. Finally, they didn't have enough space to put all the kids' stuff even in the two rooms, so they were building a new wing on the house.

And they had flat-out run out of money. They were at their wits' end, but not far enough out at their wits' end. They still weren't thinking about how to change things; they were trying to find a way to rebudget, to take on extra jobs, to find something more that they could refinance or mortgage or use as collateral for a loan. They wanted to know if there was any way they could get more credit cards. It simply hadn't occurred to them that they could change their behavior.

Their kids responded to all of this by demanding more and more and pouting if they didn't get everything they asked for—"You don't love us enough. If you loved us enough, you'd get it for us."

I was reminded of the classic Ray Bradbury story "The Veldt." In it, there's a family that has everything, and they've bought their kids the ultimate adventure playground—a holographic, virtual reality room in which the kids can create any environment they want just by imagining it. Their favorite is an African veldt, complete with wild animals.

Finally, the parents decide that this is too much— their kids are too spoiled and growing too out of touch with reality. They forbid them to use the room anymore and decide to sell the house and start over on a more modest scale. That night, the kids trick the parents into entering the room and lock the door on them.

When the real estate agent comes the next morning, the children inform her that their parents aren't home.

Meanwhile, in the playroom, the lions are plucking the last shred of meat from two fresh carcasses.

Ron and Marge's story had a happier ending. Interestingly, while this was the most out-of-control case I ever worked on, it wasn't the most difficult. Although they didn't know they knew it, everyone in the family really knew that they didn't want things to be the way they were. Everyone—the kids included—was waiting for someone to tell them, "You have to change. You can change. And this is how you can change."

I sat down with the whole family, and we worked out a budget. This is pretty basic stuff, but it was new to Ron and Marge. They weren't stupid people, but they did not know that you could put any budgetary expense ahead of your children, or that you could talk about money or financial problems in front of your kids.

We started with priorities: taxes, mortgage, utilities, car payments. We worked down through immediate needs and long-term needs, like college savings. Toys and "stuff" were last. The kids started to wail, but I looked straight at them and asked, "Is there anything on this list that you think toys should go ahead of?"

They looked at each other, at their parents, at the list *carefully*, and back at me. "No," they said.

We agreed that the budget could handle $100 each for Christmas presents for the kids, and the kids accepted this.

And at this point, it was as if some sort of invisible chain had been broken. If buying more and more, getting more and more, lost its hypnotic hold on the family, so did accumulating more and more. The kids, on their own, decided to go through their old stuff, identifying everything that they no longer used or played with and donating it to a local children's hospital.

The family started a new Christmas tradition, which they've continued to this day. Every year, they call me on Christmas Eve and gather around the phone to sing me a carol . . . and thank me.

Big Mistake #2: Shielding Your Kids from the Cost of Things

One of the things that got Ron and Marge into so much trouble was the idea that you have to shield your kids from the harsh realities of money. "We don't want to take their childhoods away from them," they told me.

I've heard of similar problems from people who grew up in households that were relatively comfortable. "You just didn't talk about it. You didn't ask how much things cost. Polite people simply don't discuss it."

Tad, when he was courting his lovely wife, Pat, recalls going out for dinner with her and her son:

"Dustin was 8 years old then, and I remember a couple of things from my early days of getting to know these people who would become so central to my life. One was the day I found myself explaining to him that 'a long, long time ago there was a singer named Elvis who was very famous.' Another was that when we went out to dinner together, he always wanted to look at the check when it came.

"At first I was outraged. It was rude. Kids don't do that. And I was probably stuck enough in my economic Victorianism that I said something like 'If you're not paying the check, it's no business of yours.'

"But I did come to realize that was old baggage I was carrying around. And I hadn't even met Neale yet, to have her teach me the error of my ways. I had to figure it out for myself: Why shouldn't he know about the world around him?

"So I got over it, and I started letting him look at the check. It did him no harm, and it may have done me some good, because sometimes he caught errors in it."

Anything that involves money, and exchange of value, can be used as a learning tool. If your kids are looking at the check, you can explain what the tax is and how it's calculated.

You can explain how to figure a tip and why you leave one. Explain the economics of being a waiter or waitress, and how much a part of their necessary income is derived from tips.

For younger kids, with whom you're still doing math games, this can be fun and educational. But it's important in different ways for kids who have outgrown the math-game stage. If you haven't explained yet about tipping to your teenagers, you need to, and I'll be devoting a more detailed section to it later on.

Shielding your children from the cost of things can keep them from getting a good start on their own—and, in Suzette's case, can have even worse unintended consequences.

Meal Money

The lessons we learn best are the ones we teach ourselves. Give the following assignment a few times to a 13- or 14-year-old, and by the time he's 19 and off at college by himself, he's likely to be cooking a lot more of his own meals.

Here's the assignment: A meal at a casual restaurant costs $50 for a family of four—$60 with the tip. How many days could you feed the family at home for that?

Have your teenagers figure it out—make it a competition. Who can stretch the 60 bucks furthest and come up with the tastiest meals?

Suzette

Kept in the Dark

Suzette was left a widow with two teenage daughters, Jackie and Elise, when her husband died of a heart attack. Suzette was in her midfifties, and suddenly all of the financial responsibilities of the family were placed on her.

"I was totally unprepared for it," she told me. "Bill had not only handled all the family finances himself, he had kept them totally secret from me.

"This isn't one of those horror stories where the widow finds out that her husband was an embezzler or had committed suicide because he'd made bad investments and lost all his money. Bill was a good man, and he left us well provided for. He just never discussed finances with me, because he was brought up in a very conventional household where the man took all the responsibility and it was impolite to bring up the subject."

"How well?" I asked. "Was there as much as you had expected?"

"That's an interesting question," she said. "How much had we expected? I had always willed myself never to think about it. That was my defense mechanism. When Bill died, my first response was to panic and assume we were broke and would be thrown out in the streets, so I guess in that respect there was more than I had expected.

"What's really interesting is how Jackie and Elise responded. Jackie—as she told me later—had always assumed we were rich, precisely because we told her so many times, 'We can't afford it,' when she could see that we could afford a lot of things. Bill would say it be-

cause . . . well, it was what he said. I would say it because, frankly, I wasn't really doing my job as a mother.
It was easier to say, 'We can't afford it,' than to sit down
and talk about values. So right after Bill died, Jackie
went on a huge spending spree, running up more than
$6,000 in credit card bills in just a few days, until the
credit card companies started calling the house and
asking if we knew about this sudden spending spike.

"I was shocked. I thought she was being heartless
and selfish, and we had a big fight. But later, when we finally started talking about money as a family, I discovered that being kept in the dark about money had given
her a smoldering resentment. She thought that we were
millionaires, that we were always lying about 'We can't
afford it,' and that I was going to keep even more money
away from her.

"Now, after a tough period, and ultimately opening
up and sharing all our family accounts and bills and assets, Jackie has become the most farsighted and financially responsible of all of us.

"Elise was just the reverse. The day after Bill died,
Elise came home from her private boarding school. I assumed she'd come home to help out with arrangements
for the funeral, and I was touched. But when the funeral
was over, and I spoke to her about going back to school,
I discovered that she'd dropped out. She thought that we
must be flat broke, now that Bill was gone, and we
wouldn't be able to afford her tuition."

I wish I could say that Jackie and Elise are the only kids who
have been hurt by financial ignorance, but we all know that's not
true. And sometimes, teens not only don't know how much things
cost, they also don't realize that they—not their parents—will be

responsible for the costs of repairing or replacing someone else's property should they damage it. It's almost as if teens think they're coated in the financial equivalent of Teflon—"Sure, I broke it, but I'm just a kid. I don't actually have to *pay* for it, do I?" Sadly, my friend's daughter Pixie learned the hard way that her age was no excuse for her actions.

DENISE AND PIXIE

Kid Stuff It Isn't

Pixie is Denise's oldest, 17 and a high school senior in her Kansas town. She's been dating Jeremy, who's 21 and the manager of a sporting-goods store where Pixie works part-time. She's cute, smart, and vivacious, and I've always liked her. But there are some concepts that Denise and her husband were never quite able to get through to Pixie, and recently they came home to roost.

Denise called me not long ago, her voice shaking. "I'm so mad at Pixie," she said. "You won't believe what she did tonight."

Pixie and Jeremy had been breaking up and getting back together with some regularity. And on this particular evening, Pixie and her friends drove by Jeremy's house and saw his former girlfriend's car outside.

"On some crazy whim, they decided to 'teach her a lesson'—why her and not him, I don't know," she said. "But they got some gloppy stuff—peanut butter, shaving cream, petroleum jelly, and I don't know what all—and covered her entire car with it, including going inside and doing the steering wheel and dashboard. Then I'm afraid it got worse. One of the girls took an ice pick and punctured all of her tires."

"Don't volunteer to pay for any of the damages," I told her.

"I know," she said. "But Pixie is refusing to pay for them either. She says it's all Jeremy's fault, and he should pay for them."

There was a standoff in Denise's house for a couple of days, compounded by her two younger brothers vociferously standing up for Pixie. "Yeah! Yeah, make him pay!"

Meanwhile, the cost of the spree was skyrocketing. In addition to the tires, the ice pick had hit some of the body. And the glop on the steering wheel had gotten smeared over some of the upholstery. ("But those were accidents! They're not my fault!" "Yeah, those were accidents! They're not Pixie's fault!") The cost of repairing the car was now up around $6,000, most of it from the ice pick damage. "Well, I'm certainly not responsible for that. I didn't do it," Pixie told Denise.

Denise lost it. "So you want to dump it all on your friend, who was there to help you? You want to duck out on the responsibility and leave her twisting in the wind?"

"You always take everyone else's side against me!" Pixie yelled back, slamming the door behind her.

Pixie was still defiant, though it was starting to sound hollow when she received a summons. ("It'll be okay. Jeremy'll take care of it. He loves me, and he knows it was all his fault.") Her defiance collapsed completely, though, when the summons was delivered to her parents as well. She was dissolved in tears, but her brothers were still putting up a front.

Even their bravado collapsed, however, when the doorbell rang and two policemen were standing there, and both their sister and their mother were led away in handcuffs. The other girl had pressed charges for breaking and entering. All of Pixie's friends were arrested, too.

The criminal charges against the parents were ultimately dropped; the financial responsibility, including court costs and lawyer's fees, were not. Denise and her husband had to take out a second mortgage to pay it all off. Pixie is paying them back, but it'll take her years to do it. Pixie and her friends had to do 100 hours of community service, and the incident is on their high school records, though not on Pixie's criminal record, since she's a juvenile (two of her friends weren't so lucky).

When I sat down to talk to Pixie about all of this, I made sure that her brothers were there, too.

Here's how some of that conversation went.

"Did you know that your parents could be held liable for actions that you commit while you're still living under their roof?" I asked.

"No," said Pixie. "I thought it was just kid stuff. You don't bring people's parents into stuff like that. You don't snitch. At least . . . you didn't in junior high. And that's how I was still thinking."

"Did you know that you could be held accountable as an adult?"

"Yeah, sort of. Well, no. I thought that was just for stealing and stuff like that. You know . . . bad kids."

Big Mistake #3: Using Credit Cards to Buy Stuff for Your Kids When You Know You Shouldn't

The biggest financial danger to older teenagers—college students especially—is the credit card. The teenagers to whom the credit card is the most serious danger are the ones who suffer from a value disconnect. They don't connect things with the money it costs to buy them;

they don't connect money with the work hours it takes to earn it. When you spend money that you don't really have in order to buy something that your teenager wants—or even something that your teenager needs—you may be thinking, like Scarlett O'Hara, "I'll think about that tomorrow." When Scarlett did that, she was usually counting on herself to work, scheme, and improvise to come up with a way to get herself out of the jam she'd gotten herself into. It frequently (though not always) worked for her, but that's Hollywood.

In real life, the message you're sending to your teenager is that you can buy things without worrying about paying for them, and this is just about the worst message you can send.

JESSICA

Debt by Coffee

All through her childhood and adolescence, Jessica had heard her father laugh and say, "Well, I'll just put it on plastic and worry about it later." It always seemed to work for him, at least as far as Jessica knew. So when she graduated from high school and moved to New York to try to build a career as a film and TV sound engineer, she had no trouble at all in saying, "Well, I'll just put it on plastic and worry about it later."

By the age of 19, she had at least managed a certain symmetry to her life: She had accumulated $19,000 in credit card debt.

She knew that wasn't good, but she didn't really know how bad it was. She was starting to sort of get the idea—at least, she had started letting her answering machine take all her phone calls.

What she didn't know was how she could change it. When we first talked, she had absolutely no clue how she had gotten so far in debt, what she had done wrong. And she had no idea that there was anything she could do to change it.

Here's just one of Jessica's regular credit card charges.

She stopped by her local Starbucks every morning and afternoon for a mocha frappuccino ultra grande, at 6 bucks a pop, and charged it. That—even missing an occasional stop, which she rarely did—came to about $75 a week.

"That is a lot, isn't it?" she said. "But what can I do? I need my coffee."

"Do you know how much you're spending on coffee?" I asked.

"Sure, you just told me. Seventy-five dollars a week."

"More."

"How can it be more?"

"How much do you pay on your credit card every month?"

"Oh, I pay what they tell me to. Every month! At least almost every month."

So I ran through the numbers with her, showing her that if she continued to pay only the minimum on her bill every month, she would eventually pay off those coffees—just in time for retirement! So what was Jessica really paying for her coffee habit?

Even if you don't consider the extra she'll owe in penalties for those months when she doesn't pay—if Jessica drinks her coffee at Starbucks for 1 year, and never drinks another cup, but continues to pay the minimum on her credit cards, she'll be nearly 60 years old before she finishes paying for those mocha frappuccinos, and she will have paid approximately $15,000 in interest, which works out to more than $20 per frappuccino.

Big Mistake #4: Buying Something for Your Kids Because You Didn't Want Your Ex to Get It for Them

Kids have enough temptation to play divorced parents against each other, without putting more in their paths.

You are who you are; your ex is who he is. You couldn't change him when you were married, so you're certainly not going to change him now. If he's always wanted to be the big butter-and-egg man, don't compete with him for that role. He probably won't be able to sustain it now that he doesn't have you to play straight woman to him. And even if he does, it's the wrong competition, and it sends a very wrong message to your kids.

Divorce brings in a whole boatload of money problems, starting with the all-too-common huge disparity in income. A man's standard of living often goes up after a divorce; a woman's generally goes down, however. We all know why this happens and how unfair the disparity is. But the point here is: How do we deal with it?

Here are the big issues.

Teens Playing Parents against Each Other

It's laceratingly painful to hear your teen say, "I'm going to Dad's. He'll buy it for me. He'll let me do it."

It's a variation of "All the other kids' parents let them stay out till midnight" or "I'll be the *only* kid in my class who doesn't have her tongue pierced"—only worse. Worse because your 13-year-old can't really go and move in with the Wilsons down the block, who let their kids stay out until midnight, or with any of those myriad parents who seem to be lining their kids up at the Piercing Pagoda like lambs at a shearing station. But a teenager can ride a bicycle or bus or subway—or drive, if he's old enough—over to Dad's. Teenagers are mobile.

An Ex with Different Values and Views on Money

Throughout this book, I've been stressing the importance of sending your kids clear, consistent messages about money management. So what do you do when your ex has very different values from your own? Unfortunately, as my friend Breanna learned, kids will naturally be drawn to what they perceive as the easy, glamorous way to make a buck.

Breanna

Dad and the Dropout

Breanna and her husband came from working-class families and married young, just out of high school. Breanna worked her way through college, got her B.A., then certification as a paralegal, after which she went to work in an attorney's office.

Steve always figured that he was too smart for that—he knew how to play the angles. He embarked on a series of get-rich-quick schemes and entrepreneurial ventures, not always well thought out, and ultimately always unsuccessful. Along the way, their marriage broke up. They continued to live in the same Pacific Northwest town.

Their son, Danny, did well in school—not quite honor roll, but well enough. Then, in the spring of his junior year and in the fall of his senior year, he seemed to be showing less interest.

"I think he's cutting school a lot and hanging out with his dad," she told me. "Steve's been writing excuses for him. I've tried to talk to Steve about it, but Steve has always had this talent for not being pinned down, and he never really answers anything I ask him."

Then, a call from Breanna, boiling mad.

"Danny's dropped out of school," she told me. "Steve

went down with him and signed all the papers, so it's all legal and official. I called Steve, and I really lost it. I yelled at him. Steve just says that Danny wasn't really cut out for school anyway, and it should be his decision. Then he started telling me about his new business venture, how it can't miss, and that Danny will have an opportunity get in on the ground floor with him. I know he just sees Danny as a source of cheap help for him in this new business scheme—I can't believe he's really thinking of Danny's best interests. But he has Danny convinced of it. I don't know what to do!"

There wasn't much that Breanna could do at that point. And this is an extreme example in some ways, not so extreme in others.

There are some things you can't change. Breanna tried to see if she could get the dropout canceled, but she couldn't. She looked into taking Steve to family court, but even if she had won, Danny would have missed so much school by the time a verdict was handed down that he wouldn't have been able to graduate anyway.

More generally than that, here's the point. If you have irreconcilable differences with your ex, there's not much chance that you'll be able to reason with him at this point on very many of your differences about values, even when it comes to something that should be a common concern, like child rearing.

The only thing you can do is stick to your principles and values. Breanna doesn't tell Danny that he's a bad person for having made his choice, and she doesn't tell him that Steve's a bad person either.

But lately, Danny has begun talking to her. Steve's can't-miss business venture is starting to fall apart. Danny told Breanna that it wasn't Dad's fault—some guys were cheating him. . . . All the contracts were going to minorities because of affirmative action (there is no affirmative action program for the awarding of contracts to minorities in their state). . . . It was the economy. Breanna had heard all the stories before, but she didn't tell Danny that.

Instead, Danny started to figure it out for himself. And then he asked Breanna about going with him to register for getting his GED.

"I told him I thought that was a wonderful thing to do," Breanna said. "But he was capable of doing it himself, and he could go and do it."

Breanna's insistence on Danny taking responsibility for himself paid off. He did find out the requirements for a GED, studied for it, and passed it. Last fall, he enrolled in a local community college.

When dealing with your ex, the only line that you can take is "my house, my rules." Make sure that your own values are consistent and that you feel right about them, and then stick to them.

What if your ex has a lot more money than you do and a more affluent lifestyle? There may be problems that you'd expect, such as your teen seduced by the lure of affluence. And there may problems you might not expect. You may need to reassure your teen that you're all right, that he needn't worry about you having less.

This connects back to being open with your teen about money and budgeting. If you take a matter-of-fact attitude about money, and you don't romanticize it *or* put it down, then you should be able to make your teen understand that just because you don't have a boat, it doesn't mean you're a pitiable creature or a candidate for the poorhouse.

Habits of Other Extended-Family Members

If you think your ex is a problem, what about your former in-laws? If they're bound and determined to win your child's affection with gifts, there's probably not a darn thing you can do about it, except not get into a competition with them.

But sometimes there are even more insidious problems. Like your own parents.

Carol Ann

"Grandma says I don't have to work."

Carol Ann, the mother of a teenage boy, recently discovered that the money-management skills she was carefully teaching her son were being undermined by a surprise gift from her mother.

"It's wonderful to know that your parents care enough to set up a trust fund for their grandchildren. But what if they don't tell you about it? When my son Alex was 14, he suddenly started walking around with a smug 'I've got a secret' look on his face and 'Never you mind' answers when we asked him about it.

"Well, a 14-year-old can't keep a secret for all that long, and eventually he let us in on the secret. He had money of his own, from Grandma and Grandpa, and he didn't have to work.

"What? He darn well did have to work. We were Neale Godfrey parents. We'd read *Money Doesn't Grow on Trees* and *A Penny Saved,* we'd had him using the Jar System for saving and a work-for-pay allowance. We've always believed in it, and we still do.

"'Grandma says I don't have to work,' Alex said defiantly. 'I have a truss fun, and when I get to be 18, I can spend it any way I want to!'

"I went and talked to my mother, and I found out, to my horror, that it was true. She had set up a trust fund for Alex, it came due when he was 18, and there were no strings attached.

"Now, I should make it clear that my husband and

I aren't like those parents of child TV stars you read about, the ones who take all the kids' money and spend it on themselves. And if Mom wants to leave all her money to Alex, that's fine with me, too. Bill and I work hard, we make a comfortable living, and we don't need to be taken care of. But this was so irresponsible. How could she have not told us?

"'You never let me do anything for Alex,' she said. 'You won't even let me buy him anything for Christmas.'

"We had asked Mom to put a monetary ceiling on how much she spent for Alex's Christmas and birthday presents—one that she was not scrupulous about sticking to. And last Christmas, we'd made her return the gift she got him, not just because it was too expensive but also because it was an all-terrain vehicle, and those things are a serious accident waiting to happen, in the hands of a 13-year-old.

"I'm hoping I can convince her to rewrite the terms of the trust so that it goes for Alex's college education. Meanwhile, Alex is still working a summer job and dividing up his money using the Jar System. Our house, our rules."

Big Mistake #5: Spending Money on Your Kids and Not Letting Your Spouse Know

Most of us, for one reason or another, grow up being secretive about money, and that's part of the story here. The other part relates to value disconnect. If you can hide it from someone, it didn't really happen.

You know you don't want your kids to learn lessons of deception. And you don't want to put them in the position of conspiring with one parent against the other. But it can happen.

Amy

"Don't tell Mommy."

Amy, whom we met in chapter 1, recalls how her now ex-husband used to make her the bad guy when money ran short. Even worse, he'd bring the kids into the deception.

"I think Jake somehow believed that if I didn't know that money was being spent, it wasn't really being spent. As long as he didn't have to think about it—and mostly, he didn't. When he was out of work and I was working, and he'd get phone calls from creditors, even then he could avoid thinking about it, because he'd just tell them, 'My wife will have to call you back.' Then when I would say, 'We're out of money,' he was always incredulous. He'd look at me accusingly and say, 'Where did it go?' like I was spending it all. Which I was, actually . . . on bills.

"But in order to complete the self-deception, it got to the point where he was bringing the kids into the conspiracy, buying them things and telling them not to tell Mommy. So I'd find a toy, a CD, or a sweater that I'd never seen before, and the kids would get all nervous and say they didn't know where it came from. That's when I knew things were going too far."

Big Mistake #6: Spending Money on Your Kids and Not Letting Yourself Know

According to a recent study done by Ohio State University for the U.S. Department of Labor, the average teenager gets $50 a week in disposable income from parents, above and beyond any money the teen gets as allowance. This is just the money that parents hand out in dribs and drabs without realizing it: five bucks here, three bucks there. And it can be a lot more that that, too. Kids from affluent families—those with incomes of $100,000 or more—frequently get as much as $175 a week in unaccounted-for "pocket change."

That's not a shabby salary for doing nothing. It comes out to a potential $9,000 a year.

The way to find out if you're doing this—and very many American parents do it much more than they think they do—is by keeping a No-Magic-Money Log for a few weeks to find out just how much money you actually do give your kids.

In order to make the count accurate, you have to be sure that you actually control every transaction that involves money leaving parents' hands and going into kids' hands. Make sure that your

Keeping a No-Magic-Money Log

It's easy. A No-Magic-Money Log is based on the simple theory that every penny of your money gets spent for something, and if you keep a record of everything you spend, you'll know exactly where all of it went.

So get yourself a little spiral memo pad, a stack of index cards, or a Palm organizer, and every day write down everything you spend, no matter how inconsequential. This includes money that you give to your kids. Write down the date, what you bought, and what you spent. No "other" or "miscellaneous" category.

Within a short time, you'll have a reviewable record that will tell you exactly where all your money goes.

This has usefulness far beyond finding out how much you're actually giving your kids. It is step one in any money-management plan.

partner is keeping his own No-Magic-Money Log. Also, make sure that your kids aren't helping themselves. And especially watch out for this: If you customarily leave your purse or wallet on the kitchen table, and your kids see it as an unspoken invitation to grab a couple of bills when they want to buy something but don't have the cash on hand, then make sure that custom gets changed.

It's important to know how much money is actually passing through your hands and into your kids' hands, but it's also worthwhile to know the dynamics of these transactions. Do you ask your teen what he needs the extra 10 bucks for, or do you just fork it over? If you do ask, are there sob stories that are more or less likely to work on you? This can happen. The sports-loving dad may be more likely to fork over the asked-for cash if it's to buy sports equipment or to see a game.

A No-Magic-Money Log is a way of getting to know yourself better. When you write down the donation to your teen's slush fund, note what it's earmarked for. If it's "Oh, just stuff," write that down. At least you'll know how much you're willing to give up for "just stuff."

But ultimately, "just stuff" is never a satisfactory accounting for how money is spent. Your goal in any No-Magic-Money Log is to reduce the amount of "just stuff" money to nothing and to account for everything.

When you go over a few weeks' worth of your log, you may find other patterns. Are you most likely to give a little extra to your teen on payday or just before supper or on a Sunday morning?

You didn't realize that? You can bet your teen knows it.

Big Mistake #7: Not Knowing What Your Kids Spend Their Money On

Do you need to know where your kids' money goes? Isn't it an invasion of your kids' privacy?

The answer to this one is the answer to so many things: Use your own good common sense. You don't have to make them account for every penny; that's not the point. But you should have a good general idea of their spending habits.

If you know what your kids spend their own money on, you'll know what they value. You'll know how they're changing, what kind of people they're growing into.

You should know if your teen is spending too much . . . or perhaps hoarding too much.

You may be able to anticipate problems—or recognize some of them early on. An important tip: Pay very close attention if your teenager starts to spend more money than he legitimately ought to have.

MARISA

A New Wardrobe? Maybe. But a New Rolex?

This story doesn't have a happy ending. Marisa was in denial beyond anyone whom I'd ever seen. Her son, Jameson, 16 years old and a student at a New York City private school, suddenly began wearing a brand-new wardrobe of expensive clothes. He came from an affluent social stratum, but this was to the extreme: Armani suits, Dolce and Gabbana jeans, accessories by Prada and Gucci.

He was obviously dealing drugs, but Marisa wouldn't see it. He told her he had a part-time job developing Web sites. Since Marisa was Internet-illiterate, she had no way of verifying this and no way of knowing that Jameson's entire Web experience consisted of finding porno sites.

When her friends tried to warn her, she indignantly told them that her son had a great eye for bargains—he'd learned it from her. She told us that there was nothing wrong with Jamie; he was a good boy, and he was popular. He had lots and lots of friends. In fact, they stopped by the apartment all the time, sometimes just for 15 to 20 minutes to see him and say hello. And different friends all the time!

Finally, Jameson was seen sporting a $10,000 Rolex. When we talked to Marisa about it, she asked Jamie and was told that it was a knockoff he'd bought on the street. Great copy, eh?

This time we really pressured her. Finally, she took the watch out of her son's room and went to a jeweler. What was it worth? Ten thousand bucks. And they don't come discounted.

Jameson's response, when Marisa confronted him, was to get furious with her for going into his room and invading his privacy.

She has him in therapy now. How much that will help, her friends don't know.

PART 2

What Kids
Don't Know Can
Hurt Them—And You

4

INTRODUCING YOUR TEENS TO FAMILY FINANCES

Here are some typical things that kids have heard about family finances.

- "We can't afford it."

- "We're in trouble."

- "We'll always take care of you."

- "We can't afford it. . . . Well, okay, just this once."

- "We want you to have the best."

- "We can't afford it. . . . Well, okay, we'll charge it and take care of it later.

Financial Literacy for Teens

The Jump$tart Coalition for Personal Financial Literacy reports that teenagers' financial knowledge is in rapid decline.

44.2 % of high school seniors got a failing grade in financial literacy in 1997

59.1 % failed in 2000

68.1 % failed in 2002

10 hours of training are thought to have a profound impact on the way kids handle money

For information on starting a financial literacy program in your community, get in touch with the Morris County Chamber of Commerce. Its program, called Business and Education Together Foundation, brings local professionals in to guide and judge the creation of business plans by high school juniors and seniors. The address is 25 Lindsey Drive, Suite 105, Morristown, NJ 07960, and the phone number is (973) 539-3882.

In other words, they've received very mixed messages, which essentially means they know nothing.

Here are some of the specific things that kids don't know.

How Much Their Parents Make

We live in a world in which immense sums are floated around the media, and they're pretty much the only salaries your kids hear about. A hundred million dollars for baseball player Mike Piazza. Forty million for Pierce Brosnan to play James

Bond. A hundred million for rapper Eminem. Oprah Winfrey makes $250 million a year.

So a lot of kids think that their parents make a whole lot more than they do. They know Mom doesn't make anywhere near what Oprah makes. But if Oprah makes $250 million, Mom can't be making any less than half a million, can she?

Here's what some kids I talked to believe that their parents make, followed by the real amount.

TREVOR, AGE 17

Trevor's dad started his own computer consulting firm in Morristown, New Jersey, 7 years ago. Before that, he worked for IBM. His mom doesn't earn a salary. Trevor is the oldest of three kids.

"Dad earns . . . well, I don't have a clue . . . about $350,000."

Fact: Dad actually earns a base of $100,000 with a bonus opportunity of $150,000, which means that he could conceivably take in a gross of $250,000 in a given year, but in reality it's likely to be a great deal less than that. Since he's had the business, he has never taken even one-half of the maximum bonus.

Trevor had a rude awakening early in his senior year of high school when he got applications to Princeton and Swarthmore, and his parents broke the news to him that there wasn't enough money for him to go to a private college.

"I'm so mad at my parents that I can't even talk to them," he told me. "I thought all parents just automatically saved for their kids' college."

I know something about Mike and Jen's finances, and I explained them to Trevor. When he was born, they made the decision that Jen would stay home and take care of the kids. And when their two other children were born, it seemed even more of a priority. They were able to make do on Mike's salary and even save a little. But when the opportunity to start his own business came up 7 years ago, they needed those savings to help with the start-up costs.

Mike started the business in 1995, just as the demand for computer high-tech services was really starting to roll. He paid himself $100,000 a year. This was enough to meet his basic expenses, which included a $300,000 mortgage and the repayment of a $200,000 loan he had taken out to start the business. He couldn't expect to take advantage of the bonus opportunity during the first 3 years, but in the 4th and 5th years, he gave himself a $50,000 bonus, which meant he went up into a higher tax bracket, so they didn't see all that much of the bonus.

By the 6th year, the high-tech boom was over, and he was struggling to keep afloat. He could pay himself the basic $100,000 salary, but no more. Now nearing age 50, Mike realized that putting money in a retirement SEP (simplified employee pension) IRA was becoming more and more of priority.

Mike had taken something of a gamble with Trevor's college fund. His long-term strategy was that by Trevor's junior year in high school, Mike would be able to invest in a 529 Plan, whereby parents can put away $110,000 in 1 year for a child's college education—tax-free for as long as the money stays in the plan, and with federal tax-free distributions to pay for the beneficiary's college costs. It might have worked if the bottom hadn't fallen out of the tech market.

When I explained all of this to Trevor, he was silent for a few moments and then said this: "I'm really proud of my dad for starting his own business and making a go of it. And I'm really grateful that Mom decided to stay home with us when we were growing up—I wouldn't trade it for anything. And I'm glad they decided to buy this house. I love living here. And if there is any extra money, I'd want it to go into Mom's and Dad's retirement. They deserve it. The state colleges here in New Jersey are terrific. And I work part-time, so I make my own spending money. The bottom line is, I'll be okay.

"But why couldn't they have told me? I would have understood. Why did they let me go on thinking there was money for Princeton, and then suddenly spring it on me?"

DAWN, AGE 15

Dawn is from a blended family—two kids from each previous marriage, making four in all.

"Dad was a chiropractor but isn't working now. We must not have any money at all, but Mom and Dad don't talk about it. I'd like to ask them about it, but I don't know how. So I just don't sleep much anymore from worrying."

Dawn didn't mention that Mom works as an office temp, probably because she can't imagine that it amounts to anything, since it's part-time and temp work. But because of her high-level skills as an executive secretary, she makes more than Dawn thinks. Dad is living off a trust fund that comes from an inheritance from his father while he tries to write his novel, but he's never told the kids about it. Between the office temping and the trust fund (one source of income Dawn underestimates and one that she doesn't know about), the family lives on about $60,000 a year.

HARRIS, AGE 14

"Mom is a director of marketing at a major e-learning company, and Dad is a teacher. I would guess that together they must make $1,000,000 a year."

Mom's company is having problems because of the economy, and all executives are taking half their salaries and no bonus this year. So, this year Mom will earn $150,000, and Dad will earn $72,000.

DANA, AGE 17

"Dad is a plumber, and Mom is a waitress. Dad earns $17 an hour and puts in a lot of overtime. Mom's salary is small, but she gets good tips."

After a little math, Dana figured out that together they earn about $55,000 a year. She was within $1,000 of their actual take-home income last year.

When I told Dana this, she looked quietly proud of her knowledge.

"Do your parents talk to you about family finances?" I asked.

"Yeah," she said. They're honest with me, and they tell me what they think I need to know. I want to help them out, and I know the best way I can do that right now is to keep getting good grades so I can get a college scholarship."

How Much the Basic Household Expenses Are

This is the other half of the Basic Ignorance Daily Double: "We can't afford it" is a meaningless phrase all by itself, and frankly, so is knowing the parents' income. If a child thinks his parents make $250,000 a year, and he discovers that they make only $50,000, that can be a rude shock and even instill a little terror. But, ultimately, the important thing is only how this affects decision making in the family.

RON AND MARGE AND ETHAN AND BILLY

A Window-Shopping Spree

Ron and Marge's two sons were 13 and 12, which meant their interests lay squarely between Toys "R" Us and Modell's Sporting Goods store, so I took them to both stores one day.

I asked them to window-shop for everything they wanted. I told them to take a notebook and write down everything they wanted and then list next to it the price of the item. I actually had to show them how to read a price tag, because this was a skill they had never had to learn.

When they were finished, we sat down over a Coke and a pocket calculator and totaled up everything they wanted. It came to $15,000.

I pointed out to them that their parents made $35,000 a year.

They were silent for a moment as they did the math, and then Ethan smiled.

"Hey, that's less than half, then," he said. "They still have plenty of money left over for themselves."

Look Who's Spending Now

According to *American Demographics* magazine, in 1980 American children ages 4 to 12 influenced about $50 billion of their parents' purchases. By 2001, that figure, fueled by a combination of aggressive marketing to children and the myth—not dispelled by parents—of bottomless pockets, had rocketed to $300 billion.

Some other things that kids generally don't know about the basics of household expenses include how a family budget is prioritized and how bills are paid.

All of these numbers have to be put into context. They don't mean anything by themselves.

The family finance sheet on the opposite page can help you understand how much—or how little—they know. When you ask them to fill it out, have some fun with it. Make it a game. These are all questions for which very few kids come even remotely close to knowing the answers, and you'll want to reassure your kids that they aren't disgracing themselves by their ignorance.

How Much the Family Has Saved

If your kids don't know how much you have saved, they probably have an inflated idea of your savings, like Trevor, who assumed that all parents saved enough to pay for their kids' college educations.

It's not your job to scare your kids to death, but it is your job to prepare them for the realities of the world. There may not be enough money for an Ivy League college. There may not be enough for a lot of extras.

Teen's Family Finance Estimate Sheet

Try this exercise on your teenage kids. First, just have them sit down and do it, with no research or help from you—the point of the exercise is to determine what they think and how far their expectations are from reality. Later, you'll compare their estimates with the real figures. Have each of your kids do this separately, without consulting with the others.

	Teen Estimate	Actual Figure
How much do you think we make a year?		
How much do you think our basic monthly expenses are?		
How much do you think we pay in taxes?		
How much do you think we save?		
How much do you think we give to charity?		
What other basic monthly expenses do you think we have? (List them all.)		
How much do you think is left over?		

There are three reasons that many adults don't discuss the family's larger financial picture, including savings, with their kids.

First is the misguided belief that we need to let kids be kids, that it's best to shield them from the harsh realities of life. This is just wrong, as I've said over and over again. Scare them to death? No. Let them know that whatever happens, you'll provide for them, but empower them with the knowledge they need.

Second, some parents, especially well-to-do parents, feel that they have to hide their total worth from their kids, for fear that if the kids know their parents have $100,000 in savings, they'll want new mountain bikes every week. But the kids need to understand the family's total picture. If you're fortunate enough to be wealthy, you have a different set of challenges, ones that aren't going to be lessened by pretending to your kids that you're hard up for money. They know you're not. And if there is enough money for a mountain bike every week and a new catamaran every summer, then your kids have to know why they aren't getting it and what service, responsibility, and, yes, *noblesse oblige* mean.

For the rest of us, there's more likely to be a third reason that we don't discuss finances with our kids: We don't tell them how much we've saved, because we're embarrassed by how little it is.

Frankly, this is no reason to hold back—in fact, it's a tremendously strong reason why you should open up. You don't want a savings shortfall to come as a sudden, rude shock to your kids, as it did for Trevor.

More than that, if you're not saving, it's because you're spending—probably more than you should be. And quite likely, you're spending more on short-term wants for your kids than you should, at the expense of long-term needs. And just as likely, if you sat down with your kids and discussed the big picture, they'd be more than happy to help design a budget that omits some of those short-term wants.

Your kids also need to know—and so do you—that your first

Alan Greenspan Says . . .

Federal Reserve Chairman Alan Greenspan recommends that everyone save 10 percent of annual earnings. The average American family saves or invests about 4 to 6 percent of their household income. By contrast, the average Japanese family saves 16 percent.

savings priority, the first savings priority of any adult, is your own retirement. Your kids are better off working their way through college now than having to worry about supporting you later, when they have their own kids to take care of.

The Bottom Line

How much should your kids know about your financial situation overall? There really isn't much they shouldn't know.

If you're wildly rich—well, if you're wildly rich, you probably have your own army of financial advisors at your beck and call and don't really need my advice, but here it is anyway—make sure your kids know that they still have to work for what they want (including a work-for-pay allowance) and that they have a responsibility to contribute to the world into which they have been born so fortunate.

If you're at the lower end of the income scale, your kids really have to know what's there. They have to know what, if anything, you'll be able to contribute to their college education and how much they'll have to come up with themselves.

For most of us in the middle, of course, that's equally important. None of us will be able to breeze through paying for college.

The real question is, what shouldn't you tell your kids about your financial situation?

You don't have feel as though you need to consult with them about or justify to them everything you buy for yourself. If you include your kids in your family budget planning and bill paying, you'll be letting them know that a part of your income goes to your own discretionary spending. If they start kvetching, "How come you get more discretionary spending money than we do?" it's easier to nip this in the bud when everything is in the open. And if your kids are grumbling under their breath, "How come Mom goes to a day spa once a month, and she doesn't pay for us to have personal trainers?" and they're in the dark about the family finances, that's going to present more of a long-term problem than if it's discussed now.

If you're in financial difficulties, perhaps facing a serious cutback in your lifestyle (such as selling the house and moving to a smaller one, or having to take on a second job), perhaps even facing bankruptcy, then your kids need to know, in general, what the situation is. They don't, however, need to become part of a cycle of hysteria. You don't need to take a daily temperature reading of how close you are to the poorhouse and send out bulletins at every meal. If family belt tightening is needed, your kids should know, and they should know what sacrifices they'll have to make. But you should reassure your kids that feeding them, clothing them, keeping a roof over their heads, and educating them will always be your first priority.

5

MONEY AND LIFESTYLE: WHAT TV DOESN'T TELL THEM

How do people live out on their own in the big world? What do kids know about the way that young adults live in their first apartments, with their first jobs, negotiating their first budgets? Mostly, they know what they see on TV, which means they are being misled, to say the least.

Living the TV Life

How exactly does Jack on *Will and Grace* afford his nice apartment—not to mention his clothes? How does Kramer pay the rent? Television is full of shows that convince teens that it must not be very difficult for young adults to live well on their own.

Charmed

Here we have three sisters living in a mansion-size house in a very posh San Francisco neighborhood. The house is an inheritance and presumably mortgage-free (at least they never mention a mortgage)—a nice trick if you can pull it off.

But even given that the Halliwell sisters have no basic shelter costs, they'd still have a fair amount of upkeep on a house that size, not to mention utility bills and taxes.

But the biggest expense for the Halliwell sisters must be home decorating, given that every week furniture gets destroyed, fixtures get pulled out of the walls, and their home sustains varying degrees of structural damage. I don't know if their insurance covers it— most homeowner policies don't cover acts of God, but they may have different clauses regarding acts of demons. If so, I would hate to think what the Halliwell sisters' premiums look like.

How do they pay for all this? One of the sisters runs a disco, but it can't be making much money for them, because an operation like that needs hands-on attention, and she's hardly ever there. One of them is married. Now, we don't want to teach our daughters that some white knight, or White Lighter, is going to come along and take care of them, but in this case, her husband is essentially an apparition, which would make it difficult for him to get a steady paying job. The third writes an advice column, which pays about $50 a week unless you write the "Dear Abby" column.

Friends

This may be the champion of all role models for teenagers imagining what it would be like to be young adults living on their own, sharing apartments, and partaking in big-city life. The series and its characters have gone through a number of permutations since it started, but in the early days there were two men—a computer specialist who worked on and off and an aspiring actor who rarely worked—and two women, a chef who worked on and off and a waitress who worked steadily but in a bottom-of-the-economic-barrel job.

Each group lived in a roomy upper East Side apartment—in an older building, probably a walk-up, but, still, the rent on each of those apartments had to be at least $3,500 a month.

What's the message we get from *Friends* about moving away from home? Maybe that there's no real connection between how or whether you earn a living and where you live. You can live like your friends just by being friends with them.

Buffy the Vampire Slayer

Sometimes even a TV fantasy can yield surprising insights. Take this episode of an old favorite of teens that's now in syndication, *Buffy the Vampire Slayer*.

Buffy's mother died recently. Actually, so did Buffy, but she's been brought back to life by a series of spells and incantations, only to find out that sometimes it's better to be dead. Not so much because she has to battle the demon who's been brought to life with her, but because she suddenly discovers that she's the head of the household, the plumbing is shot, and there's no money to pay the bills.

One of her friends suggests that she start charging a fee for saving the world, but Buffy's quite sure that she can't do that. ("Spider-man does," her friend argues, but the rest of the group disabuses her of this notion.)

Buffy goes to apply for a loan, but she's woefully unprepared. She thinks that she has to prove that she's a good person, so she takes in things like the junior high school report card on which she got straight A's. The loan officer has to explain to Buffy that the only thing that matters is collateral. She doesn't have any. She has her house, but it's not amortized.

As it happens, while she's there a demon bursts into the bank, and Buffy vanquishes him (not before his henchmen have robbed the bank). She succumbs to the temptation of trying to make a buck off her calling, but it's "no go." Having driven a demon out of the bank is no substitute for collateral.

Giles, Buffy's watcher and older friend, arrives back in town (he'd left because he figured he was no longer needed after Buffy's demise). The fearless slayer, who thinks nothing of prowling vampire-infested streets, crypts, and subterranean passageways, confides in him that money problems are getting the better of her. She's trying not to think about it, but she wakes up at 4:00 A.M. terrified.

Giles recognizes that his protégé is facing a real-world problem unlike any she's had to deal with before. "Life can be pretty overwhelming even for people who haven't been trapped in a hell zone," he assures her. "Tomorrow we'll go over all the bills."

The demon intervenes, breaking into her house for a pitched battle, during which Buffy, for the first time, finds herself moving furniture out of the way, saving vases and bric-a-brac. She lures the demon into the basement and away from the furniture, but as the battle nears its climax, the demon fuels her anger (and seals his fate) by tearing down her new copper pipes.

"I trashed this house so many times," she wails. "How did Mom pay for all this?

"I don't think I can do this," she confesses as she sits down with Giles and the books.

"Yes you can," he tells her kindly but sternly. "You just go from crisis to crisis. Your mother did it all the time—and without the aid of any superpowers."

Giles's last piece of advice isn't the best. A real-life superhero mom will do more than go from crisis to crisis, and without any superpowers (granted, with a daughter like Buffy, it must have particularly hard for Mrs. Summers to stay ahead). And if you're watching a show like this with your teen, it's not a bad idea to mention this while still commending Giles's basic point. A show like this can really open up a dialogue, and a line like "I trashed this house so many times. How did Mom pay for all this?" may hit home for both parent and teen.

A Dose of Reality

Actually, on a handful of shows the realities of making a living get a more honest treatment—starting, perhaps, with *Smallville,* where young Clark Kent still lives at home with his parents, who deal with the realities of running a small farm. One suspects that when Clark does leave home, he'll take care of getting a day job first—perhaps as a newspaper reporter, which is a union job with a good health plan and retirement benefits—before he turns his attention to fighting crime.

A teenage friend, Murray, pointed out to me that some very good attention to the realities of life for young adults can be seen on *Scrubs,* which features young doctors and nurses working in a big-city hospital. The series sends the message that just because you're a doctor, it doesn't mean you're rolling in money. The first-

Young Doctors in Debt

According to data from the Association of American Medical Colleges, 1999 medical students owed an average of $90,745 in educational debt. And 13.9 percent of indebted students owed $150,000 or more—a figure that had jumped from 8.1 percent in just 2 years.

If she takes out student loans for all of her med school education, the average American doctor will be 43 years old before she starts making a profit on her education.

year residents are constantly in a struggle to make ends meet, and some of them have to work second jobs. One story line involved the resident who was being supported by money from her daddy, on the condition that she specialize in the field he wants her to. She chooses not to, he cuts her off, and she comes to understand the problems the others have, as she has to look for a cheaper apartment and a second job.

"But I tell you, Neale, that show really opened my eyes," Murray told me. "I suddenly realized that life isn't like *Friends.* Everything costs money out there, and just because you're a doctor, it doesn't mean it's all going to be a red carpet. I'm planning to go to med school, and frankly, I'd always somehow assumed that I'd get my diploma, the keys to a Porsche, and a high-rise apartment. My mom's a doctor, and, after watching that *Scrubs,* I asked her what it was like starting out and got an earful. It made me feel closer to her, and it made me realize I've got an awful lot to learn."

Budgeting in the Real World

Here are a few questions you may want to try out on your teenager.

- How much do you think it costs to live on your own?

- How much do you need to make to support the lifestyle you would like?

- What kind of education do you need to have to make that much?

Don't be surprised at what you hear. Listen to my conversation with Jessica, a young adult who's already out on her own and still can't even answer those questions.

"I don't know. . . . I never added it up. The bills come in and I pay them . . . sort of."

"What is sort of?" I ask.

She giggles. "Well, I pay the ones I open. I just put them on plastic."

"And when do you pay that?"

"When I open it."

Jessica stops giggling and starts snuffling a little. "I never thought about adding it up. I just figured it all works out somehow."

"How did you decide what kind of apartment you could afford?"

"I just rented one I liked."

"What kind of job do you think you'd need to afford this apartment?"

Now she's sobbing. "I don't know! What kinds of jobs do Monica and Phoebe and Rachel have? And they all get by."

Facing Reality

Here's the best way to bring your teen out of the land of TV and into reality. First, ask him to choose the way he imagines himself living 2 years, then 5 years, then 10 years out of college (or high school, if he's thinking of not going to college). Have him choose from among the different living situations listed in the following boxes, plus high-end or low-end, where applicable. As he selects the lifestyle he'd like to live, have him enter the associated costs in the worksheet on page 84.

1. Shelter

These figures are all approximate. (We estimated them by talking to Realtors in New York and Chicago for the city numbers and consulting with Laurie Della Villa and Pat Richards of PRG Realty in New Paltz, New York, for the small-town numbers.) They represent our best estimates as of the end of 2002, and they will

Situation	Range	Approx. Cost per Month
A. Studio apartment, city	High-end Low-end	$2,500 $800
B. One-bedroom apartment, city	High-end Low-end	$3,200 $1,200
C. Two-bedroom apartment, city	High-end Low-end	$5,000 $1,800
D. Three-bedroom apartment, city	High-end Low-end	$7,000 $2,300

fluctuate at different times and in different parts of the country. But the numbers are close enough to give a teenager a general idea of what it costs to live. For shelter, high-end means the best part of town, and low-end . . . well, we're not putting your kids in an area where they won't feel safe. Let's say it's a typical, slightly down-at-the-heels college neighborhood or a moderately remote rural location. Shelter costs for most people will be somewhere in the middle.

Situation	Range	Approx. Cost per Month
E. Studio apartment, small town	High-end Low-end	$850 $400
F. One-bedroom apartment, small town	High-end Low-end	$900 $500
G. Two-bedroom apartment, small town	High-end Low-end	$1,400 $650
H. Three-bedroom apartment, small town	High-end Low-end	$1,700 $800

While these figures are just for average monthly expenses, you might remind your teenager that there are start-up costs to shelter: furniture, sheets, towels, dishes, pots, and pans. Even if he rents a furnished apartment and starts out with hand-me-down dishes and flatware from home or from yard sales, he's not likely to buy his sheets at a yard sale, and it's all going to cost something. Phones need to be installed; security deposits need to be paid.

A moving company costs money. Friends can be enlisted to help move for the cost of pizzas and soft drinks, but even then you may need to rent a truck or a van.

So the start-up costs of moving out on one's own can run anywhere from $1,000 to the-sky's-the-limit. It definitely won't come for free.

In general, the cost of utilities is included in an apartment rental, but someone who rents or shares rental on a house will have to pay his own utilities, so I'm adding them in below. These approximate figures are rent plus utilities.

For all of these situations, divide the expense by the number of residents.

Situation	Range	Approx. Cost per Month
I. One-bedroom house, small town	High-end	$1,300
	Low-end	$900
J. Two-bedroom house, small town	High-end	$1,700
	Low-end	$1,100
K. Three-bedroom house, small town	High-end	$3,000
	Low-end	$1,400
L. Four-bedroom house, small town	High-end	$3,200
	Low-end	$1,600

What if your teenager doesn't want to rent? Then discuss the living-at-home option with him and come up with a figure to fill in below. Later in the book, I'll go into more detail on the situation of a grown child living at home or moving back home, but we'll estimate for now, since there's no one way to figure this (and sometimes, because of extraordinary hardship, you'll simply be taking your child in and carrying him for a period of time). For the purpose of this exercise, figure a basic room-and-board charge of $300 a month. It's not an exorbitant figure, but it's enough to get the point across that it costs something to live at home.

To that basic figure, add the difference between your utility bills with and without your child at home. Since you don't yet know what those bills will be like with your child not there (and you'll be amazed at how much lower they'll get), figure that you'll lower your current utility costs by 20 percent with no kids in the house. This is important, because no one ever knows the value of something they've never paid for. If your teen does this exercise and suddenly sees the cost of utilities because he has to pay his share of them, you may even start seeing an immediate dividend: no more thermostat jacked up to 75 degrees so that he can wear shorts and a T-shirt around the house.

Situation	Approx. Cost per Month
M. Living at home with parents	

Suppose your teen imagines himself buying his own home? For purposes of simplicity here, let's figure this as a two-bedroom home in your community and estimate the mortgage. I've included taxes separately, because it's always worth reminding your teen that they are an expense that he'll have to bear.

Situation	Approx. Cost per Month
N. Owning own home—mortgage payment	
Utilities	
Taxes	

2. Transportation

For the cost of owning or leasing, high-end is an expensive new car; low-end, a used car. A low-priced new car would be between the two extremes. For operating costs, high-end is a lot of road trips, and low-end is a short commute and not much else. In the middle is commuting and some driving around town.

Taking cabs or public transportation assumes that your teen will be living in a city. High-end is taking cabs almost everywhere; low-end is using public transportation exclusively. In the middle would be taking the subway to work and back but using cabs at night, or living in the suburbs and taking a commuter train to work.

Again, although our figures are approximate, just doing this exercise will stimulate in your teenager the start of an awakening to what things cost. You certainly can fine-tune any of this.

You can find out about insurance costs by shopping around at a few insurance companies in your town. If you want to do some home preparation on what insurance would cost for any given car and for your teen's particular driving record, there are a number of interactive sites online, such as https://secure1.insweb.com/cgi-bin/auto.exe. Or you can do a search on Google or a similar search engine for "auto insurance cost worksheet."

It's worth stopping for a second to think about the difference between buying or leasing a top-of-the-line car and buying or leasing an economy model. That $800-a-month difference adds up to about $10,000 a year. And if you want to estimate what that comes out to when you invest it with compound interest, read "The Rule of 72" on page 235.

Situation	Range	Approx. Cost per Month
A. Own/lease your own car	High-end	$1,000
	Low-end	$200
B. Insurance	High-end	$500
	Low-end	$250
C. Operating costs	High-end	$160
	Low-end	$20
D. Cabs/public transportation	High-end	$600
	Low-end	$75

3. Food

High-end means eating out all the time, while low-end is eating at home all the time. Somewhere in the middle is getting lunch at a deli or diner but cooking dinner at home six nights a week. If your young adult-to-be is planning to have drinks with dinner regularly, she'll need to kick her estimate up a notch.

Our kids' generation didn't invent the idea of eating out as a laborsaving device. Actually, neither did our generation. My friend Lucy told me this story about her mother on Staten Island, now in her eighties. Her mom had to call in the gas company to fix a leak and was nonplussed when the service person asked if the company could buy her stove.

"You want to buy my stove? Am I hearing you right?"

"That's right, ma'am. We have a museum of gas appliances, and we've never seen a stove made in the 1940s that's still in such good condition. Why, it looks as though it's never been used!"

How about Figuring It This Way?

If you're eating out every meal, you're probably spending close to $2,500 a month, or $30,000 a year, on food. That is probably your entire yearly salary if you're a recent college graduate with a pretty good job.

So let's cut it down. If you're a little frugal with your food dollars and spend $1,000 a month, that's $12,000 a year, or 800 hours. You're working 5 months out of the year just to eat.

And if you're really careful—that is, you eat breakfast and dinner at home and brown-bag your lunch—now we're talking about 280 hours, or a little less than 2 months.

You think that's something? Ha! I was only kidding—actually, it's even worse than that. If you're a single, young taxpaying adult, you're probably taking home only about two-thirds of your paycheck. So at $1,000 a month, you're back to spending everything you earn on supporting those restaurants. And since you can't literally do that, it means you're piling up credit card debt at an alarming rate.

It starts to sound a little like the bum who comes up to a guy on the street and says, "Can I have 500 bucks for a cup of coffee?"

"But coffee only costs a dollar."

"I know, but the only place you can get a decent cup of coffee around here is the Waldorf, and I can't go there in a crummy suit like this."

If you're spending all that money on food, how are you going to pay for the nice suit to wear out to dinner?

What many teens—and adults—don't realize is that eating out regularly is wildly expensive, one of the biggest money extractors we face on a daily basis. The difference between the high and low ends on eating costs is $2,150 a month—which computes to $25,800 extra a year.

Situation	Range	Approx. Cost per Month
Average eating costs	High-end	$2,500
	Low-end	$350

4. Entertainment/Enrichment

High-end means going to clubs, attending concerts, and so forth, on a regular basis (average of once a week), or meeting friends at the local bar four or five times a week; low-end means video rentals, a magazine subscription, and an occasional movie or club night. A movie or regular lessons or classes once a week would be somewhere in the middle. This is an expense that will very much vary from person to person, and to make a budget for right now, your teen needs to know how much he's actually spending on entertaining himself. For a general sense of what the future will be like, these approximations are close enough.

Situation	Range	Approx. Cost per Month
A. Entertainment/enrichment costs, city	High-end	$1,100
	Low-end	$100
B. Entertainment/enrichment costs, small town	High-end	$700
	Low-end	$50

JESSICA

The Bar Babe

Jessica met her friends every evening after work at a local singles bar.

"Do you like going there all that much?" I asked.

"No, I hate it," she said. "It's . . . you know, it's the bar scene. Same old, same old. It's too loud. I mean, I love music and all, but they just pound you with mostly crap, and you can hardly hear yourself talk over it. And it's too smoky. And the guys there are all jerks, and you spend half your time fending off someone who wants to paw you all over."

"Do you know how much you spend there?"

"No . . . it can't be that much. I have only a couple of drinks . . . and you know, a lot of times guys buy you a drink."

"Those jerks and losers who want to paw you all over?"

Jessica giggled. "Yeah . . . actually, most of the time I'd rather buy my own drinks."

Since Jessica put everything on plastic, it was relatively easy to find out how much she spent at the bar. She wasn't a heavy drinker—no more than a couple of drinks a night for the most part; that much was true. But on the average of once a week there was a sharp spike. "You drink that much on some nights?" I asked.

"No," she said. "But sometimes I, you know, like buy a round. That's okay, isn't it? I mean, everyone else does it, too."

"Of course it's okay," I told her. "But it does cost you. You're spending around $250 a month down at Mister Mookie's."

"That much? Is that a lot?"

The figure on the plastic was pretty much the whole expense. Sadly, Jessica wasn't much of a tipper. I needed to talk to her about that, too, but it could come later.

"How do your friends feel about the bar scene?"

"Everyone hates the bar scene."

"Then why not get together at your apartment? Or different friends' apartments? Listen to the music you like at the volume you like, get rid of at least some of the smoke, pay a whole lot less for your drinks, and not have to worry about the jerks and losers."

"I don't know. I just never thought of it."

5. Clothing

High-end means wearing designer outfits—essentially, it means having a social life that requires dressing up. Low-end means your teen has a job where casual dress is acceptable, so he is wearing pretty much the same clothes at work and at home. In the middle would be having a job that requires dressing up but wearing casual clothes for social outings.

Situation	Range	Approx. Cost per Month
Average clothing costs	High-end	$1,200
	Low-end	$100

6. Health Care

Your teens need to know that health care is a major expense and that rock musicians, entrepreneurs, and freelance writers don't get it unless they pay for it themselves. So here's the way they need to figure health care. If they're working for a business, an institution, or a governmental agency that pays health benefits, it's low-end. Otherwise, it's high-end. Even if your young adult has a really good policy, it's not likely to pay for her dental care. And if she wears glasses, that's another expense that most insurance plans won't cover. And this isn't even considering medical procedures that she sees as necessary but her insurance plan sees as elective.

Situation	Range	Approx. Cost per Month
Average health care costs	High-end	$1,200
	Low-end	$100

7. Personal Expenses

This includes laundry, toilet articles, cosmetics, soap, haircuts, manicures, and so on. It's a fairly consistent expense for everyone,

Another Way of Looking at It

If you smoke 2½ packs a day, at current prices you'll spend approximately $4,500 a year on cigarettes. At the end of 10 years, that adds up to $45,000, which would be the price of a new Lexus or a down payment on a house.

If, however, you invested all that cigarette money in a fund that paid 10 percent a year, you'd have $78,440, which could buy you an antique original Tiffany Wisteria lamp, a Ferrari, or a small house in the country.

with the main difference being whether you shop at top-of-the-line boutique shops or Wal-Mart, or if you add such higher-end expenses as a personal trainer.

Situation	Range	Approx. Cost per Month
Average personal expenses	High-end	$700
	Low-end	$50

8. Personal Habits

Does your teen smoke? If she does, it's going to make a difference in her budget, and she has to figure it in. High-end here is a pack a day. Low-end means she's a nonsmoker—and congratulations. She's saved about 1,000 bucks a year, cut down on health care costs, and added 10 years or more to her life.

Smoking is probably the most wasteful and pointless of personal habits, in addition to its health issues. But a teen who spends a lot of money regularly on "extras," from high-end makeup to car detailing, is supporting a habit that has to be budgeted for.

Situation	Range	Approx. Cost per Month
Average cost of personal habits	High-end	$400
	Low-end	0

9. Emergencies and Extras

Everyone has to build into any budget some room for emergencies and extras, because they'll happen—and they'll happen all the time. Minor fender benders, medicine for the flu, a cousin coming in from out of town who has to be entertained. Figure anywhere from $50 to $200 a month for this category, depending on how independent the budgeter is.

10. Savings

Two investments in particular bring such remarkable returns that they'll make your head spin if you think about them, and neither of them involves insider trading or making a killing in the market. One is getting rid of credit card debt, and I'll discuss that in more detail in chapter 8.

The other is saving and investing money between the ages of 20 and 30. In brief, an investment of $1,000 a year, starting when your young adult is 20, will be worth about 20 times more at retirement than the same regular investment starting when he's 30. So this goes in that starting-out-away-from-home budget—without fail. Eighty-five dollars a month. Approximately one cup of Starbucks coffee a day.

11. Charity

Your teen should be able to fill in a figure here—and should want to. We need to raise our kids understanding the need to share with those less fortunate than we. It's one of the most important things we can teach them.

It's good to set a goal of 10 percent of take-home pay contributed to charity. This can include stuff as well as money. Donate books or clothing to a hospital or the Salvation Army instead of re-selling them; do the same with appliances or electronic equipment when trading up.

And make sure that your young adult remembers to contribute time, too, to volunteer organizations like Big Brothers and Sisters or Habitat for Humanity or to community projects or religious institutions. We're part of the world we live in, and it's up to all of us to make it better.

What's It All Add Up To?

Here's where your teen puts together all the information she's gathered. Have her write in her choices, along with the cost per month.

Be sure to remind your teen that the total figure, multiplied

Item	2 Years		5 Years		10 Years	
	Choice	Per Month	Choice	Per Month	Choice	Per Month
Shelter						
Transportation						
Food						
Entertainment/ enrichment						
Clothing						
Health care						
Personal expenses						
Personal habits						
Emergencies and extras		$50		$100		$200
Savings		$85		$85		$85
Charity						
Total						

by 12, is not the total amount she'll need to make each year—it's the total amount *after* taxes.

Here's a general formula for figuring out how much money gets withheld.

Income per Month	Withheld for a Single Person*
Less than $221	0
$221–$713	10%
$714–$2,471	$49.20 + 15%
$2,472–$5,402	$312.90 + 27%

*Percentage is of excess over the minimum income.

So if your young adult is making $1,500 a month, how much is being withheld? It's pretty simple with a calculator.

$1,500.00 (monthly income)
− $714.00 (minimum)
$786.00

$117.90 (15% of 786)
+ $49.20
$167.10

$1,500.00
− $167.10
$1,332.90

Where are we now? She's taking home $1,332.90 a month and feeling somewhat miffed that she'll have to recalculate her budget on the basis of slightly less money, but she doesn't know the half of it yet—and that's more or less literally true. What she's figured so far is about half of what's actually being withheld.

There are payroll deductions. There are, in most states, state taxes. Some cities have their own taxes, possibly even commuter taxes if you live there but don't work there.

For example, if your young adult lives in Illinois and makes that same $1,500 a month, her actual take-home pay, less deductions, would be:

Monthly gross pay	$1,500.00
Federal withholding	$167.29
Social Security	$93.00
Medicare	$21.75
Illinois state tax	$45.00
Net pay	$1,172.96

The calculations above come from a useful Web site, www.paycheckcity.com (you can find similar sites by doing a search on "paycheck calculator" or "income tax calculator").

Your teen needs to understand that this is what it's like out there. Decisions have to be made on the basis of a simple rule. Your personal economy is a zero-sum game. Every dollar that you spend on one thing is a dollar less that you can spend on something else.

Furthermore, every dollar that you spend on stuff is a dollar taken away from saving, and spending versus saving is *not* a zero-sum game. It's an opportunity cost game. The dollar you spend on a nice restaurant meal is always going to be that meal, that dollar. It will cost you not only the dollar, but everything else that dollar might have made, and you'll never get anything more than that meal back for it. The same dollar spent on a book may give you knowledge you can use in the future. The same dollar invested at a 10 percent return, compounded . . .

You do the math. Better yet, let your teen do the math.

6

PEER PRESSURE: KEEPING UP WITH THE JONES TEENAGERS

Teenagers have always banded together for support, comradeship, and the kind of help in negotiating the dilemmas of this world that only peers can give to each other. It's a necessary part of preparing to leave the nest and become the next generation to make its mark on the world. So peer pressure is a necessary part of growing up—and in many ways a good one. But, unfortunately, teens are all too capable of reinforcing each other's financial misconceptions. And where financial misconceptions flourish, that's where there's fertile ground for all kinds of financial mini-disasters.

Here are the six peer-pressure problems that involve money.

Peer-Pressure Problem #1:
Keeping Up with the Jones Kids

American teenagers rang in the new millennium by pushing their annual spending total up over $160 million, an increase of more than 66 percent from as recently as the mid-1990s. By 2003, it had risen to well over $170 million.

This is a market that everyone wants a piece of, and youth-oriented marketing has become very skilled—and very aggressive.

TIFFANY, AGE 14

"My friends and I mostly like to get together and watch MTV."

"Are you all music lovers?" I asked her.

"No, not really," she said. "But MTV is where you can get to see all the pretty clothes and all the pretty jewelry. We get together and watch the shows and talk about what we'd like to get and what looks really cool."

"You don't really expect to get all that stuff, do you?"

She giggled and batted her eyes. "Well . . . "

What Teens Spend Their Money On	
Clothing (jeans and sneakers)	34%
Entertainment (movies, music, consumer electronics, games)	22%
Food (fast food and groceries)	16%

Source: Interep Research

Teens want to be cool, and the one thing they're sure of is that their definition of cool doesn't match your definition. By definition. What they don't know is how much their definition is a product of manipulation.

And to some extent, they aren't going to care. It doesn't matter

And Don't Forget . . .

The ever-popular tobacco products. It seems to me that the only thing tobacco companies spend more time on than insisting they don't market to teens is figuring out new ways to market to teens.

Here's some data from the Tobacco Initiative, the Web site of the Minnesota Youth Tobacco Prevention Initiative. You decide for yourself.

• According to a July 2000 University of Illinois at Chicago study, tobacco companies have greatly increased spending in convenience stores since their billboards were forced down. . . . Studies show that three out of four teenagers shop at a convenience store at least once a week and that teens are more likely than adults to be influenced by promotional pieces in convenience stores (73 percent to 47 percent).

• The Massachusetts Department of Public Health in May 2000 found that tobacco ads in magazines with at least 15 percent youth readership (12 to 17 years old) increased by almost $30 million, or 33 percent, from the first three quarters of 1998 to the first three quarters of 1999 . . . more than a third of all tobacco magazine advertising.

• Significant increases in tobacco ads were found in magazines such as *Vibe* (42 percent teen readership) and *Spin* (32 percent teen readership).

if the "in" shoe company of the moment has spent $100 million this year to convince every teenager in the country that their old personal cross-training air-pumped, self-actualizing shoes are out and the new mystic training intense extreme shoes are in. If it's what the other kids are wearing, then it's the cool thing to wear.

Still, it's worth letting teens know the tactics that merchandisers use, because it will make some difference. No one likes to be manipulated, and teenagers, with their instinctive distrust of phoniness, least of all. So encourage a healthy skepticism in your teens. Point out to them that advertisers see teenagers as an easy mark, as a group with an unusually high penchant for spending on wants rather than needs, which makes them particularly vulnerable to hype.

In real life, not everyone's parents get them the brand-new revolutionary-design Nikes every year. And if your teen takes a close look around himself, seeing what's really there instead of what Nike wants him to see, he'll know it perfectly well.

The greatest technique of all for teaching teens that they don't need to have the latest and the coolest with the most bells and whistles is . . . a budget.

Kids have a right to expect their parents to provide them with food, shelter, and clothing. But they don't have a right to expect clothing that's more than functional. You'll provide the money for the shoes, the jeans. If they want to pay extra to turn the shoes into Doc Martens ($25 at Payless, $125 for Docs) or the jeans into Fubus ($25 at Penney's, $95 from Fubu), that's their affair—and their money.

And this isn't hard to stick to if you remember that all the rest of it is hype. You can't force your kids not to buy into it, but you don't need to encourage them, either, by paying to support their habit.

Let your kids know about the hype. And let them know just how much the world of things that they believe they've created for

---

Top of the Hype Hit Parade

According to a market analyst for Splash Plastic, a British credit card company with a strong focus on the teenage market, what's played up these days are "logos, which have low transaction values but encourage repetitive purchasing behavior."

Logos aren't just free advertising (free to the company—your teen pays through the bejeweled nose for them), they're also the principal tool the company uses to reel your teen in and create brand loyalty.

They aren't just a scam, they're a double scam.

---

themselves is the product of strategists who see your kids as pieces of meat. Tell them to do a quick Internet search on "teen marketing" if they want to see how many companies are out there analyzing them. They may even see that they are unwittingly helping these companies influence others:

> Specific teen-marketing operations aimed at the 13- to 17-year-old demographic, youth marketing is achieved by . . . online and offline recruitment of key target market influencers where trendsetters exponentially recruit members within their peer groups as well as drive consumer response. —*OnPoint Marketing*

Peer-Pressure Problem #2: Gifting It Out with (or Falling in Love with) the Jones Kids

Here's one of the really effective ways of marketing to teens, and everyone out there who wants your teenager's dollar has thought of it: young love. Valentine's Day is a hot teen-marketing day,

Christmas is an evergreen, and we won't even get into prom night.

Marketers will dream up every special day they can, but there's one they don't have to dream up: that special person's birthday. Not to mention 1-month anniversaries and 2-month anniversaries and 3-month anniversaries . . .

Teens buy into this one big time, literally and figuratively. In a newspaper advice column written by teenagers for teenagers, I came across a detailed dissertation of just how much you should spend on Christmas gifts for a beloved of various lengths of service. They laid it all out in explicit detail, from $35 for a relationship of zero to 3 months (CDs, stuffed animals, clothes), up through $200-plus for 2 years and over. The teen columnists tell you how to move from gifts of T-shirts (zero to 3 months) to sweaters and pants (3 to 6 months) to full outfits (7 to 11 months). Teen budgets and animal rights activism rule out mink coats. A CD works for the zero-to 3-month semi-significant other, and a CD player for the veteran of a 1- to 2-year relationship. Gift certificates for gradually increasing amounts are also recommended.

This is, unfortunately, the way far too many teenagers are conditioned to think. I won't even talk about the individual numbers, or even the idea of gift certificates as a present for a girlfriend, because it's the whole concept that I find so appalling. Are we negotiating a union contract here, with built-in step-increases for seniority?

The kids who wrote the column were doing the best they could to come up with a commonsense solution to a genuine teenage concern. And they were expressing an attitude that's all too common among teens—that possessions, and buying, are how you communicate.

Try this column on your teenager and see what she says. "Yeah, that makes sense" is obviously not the answer you hope for, and "That's not enough" is even worse. But "That's a little too much" is really no better. You're hoping for something along the lines of "That has nothing to do with the quality of a relationship or the spirit of Christmas."

If your teen does think that this is a reasonable prescription, ask her why. The answer "Well, at least they're trying to keep a lid on things" is actually not a bad one, because at least it recognizes a teenage problem that can get out of control—trying to out-gift each other. A relationship can spiral out of control into a battle of billfolds if each member of a teen couple is striving to be the one who spends more.

And it can spiral out of control in other ways, with cliques that make a status symbol out of the price of a significant other's gift.

We know that teens live in a world of their own, and if they get caught up in this sort of spiraling teen madness, there may little that we can do about it. Experience is a good teacher, and a 14-year-old who puts all his lawn-mowing money into a 2-week-anniversary gift for the love of his life—only to see the relationship never reach a 3-week anniversary—may turn into a sadder but wiser (and more fiscally prudent) 15-year-old. Kids learn their values from us, and from the larger society, so we want to make sure we're sending the messages that we want them to have and discussing the messages they get from others.

I've never forgotten the advice my rabbi gave when my children were tiny. "Before you step in and lay down the law, ask yourself, *Does it matter profoundly?*"

You cringe when you see all that money going into the 2-week-anniversary present, and you should comment on extravagance or a misplacement of values when you see it, but it doesn't matter profoundly. Within limits, and they're fairly broad limits, your teenager should be allowed to make his own mistakes and learn from his own mistakes with money.

And this is an area where a teen can make some pretty striking mistakes.

FRED

Love Lessons

Fred met Jeannine when they both were working at summer jobs in a national park—and it was love at first sight. He was nearly 19 and just going into his sophomore year in college, and she was just about to start her freshman year.

At the end of the summer, he went back to college in North Carolina, and she started her freshman year in northern California. But they called, chatted online, and e-mailed each other—and Fred knew this was the girl he was going to marry. He told his family. They urged caution, but they knew better than to belittle his feelings.

Fred started working a very-close-to-full-time job in addition to carrying a full load at school. Who could argue with that? Hardworking, ambitious . . . and he didn't need a social life, because he had Jeannine.

What was he doing with the money he was making? Saving it, he said. But that wasn't so. He was spending some of it on expensive presents for Jeannine and saving the rest of it to buy *really* expensive presents for Jeannine.

Jeannine loved the presents and the attention. Did she love Fred? He was sufficiently convinced of it and bought her a $2,000 diamond necklace for her birthday and a $3,000 engagement ring.

When his parents found out about this, they became really worried. They tried to tell him that he was going too fast. "There was the inevitable argument," Fred's mom, Sylvia, told me. "The one we'd been dreading, because we knew you can't talk to a boy in love. He got furious with us, told us we didn't understand anything, and stormed out.

The good part is, he didn't really go out and do anything foolish like drinking and driving—because he couldn't afford to. Every nickel he had was tied up in Jeannine."

He was flying out to California for her birthday and planned to give her both the necklace and the engagement ring. Somehow, his parents managed to convince him to take it one gift at a time—the necklace this time, the ring next time. The poor girl would be overwhelmed, they reasoned, and he accepted the theory.

As it turned out, not much would have overwhelmed Jeannine. She accepted the diamond necklace with a big smile and a kiss, and before he left, she handed Fred a note, saying, "Don't open this and read it till you get on the plane."

Yes, you guessed it. A Dear John letter—and she took the diamond necklace knowing that she had already broken up with him.

His parents tried to convince him that he should call her up and demand the necklace back, but he just said that he loved her and wanted her to have it.

He would get over that feeling soon enough—but she wouldn't have given it back to him anyway.

"It was an expensive lesson," he said. "I won't do that again."

"At least you didn't give her the ring, too," I said.

"A fat lot of good that did me," he said. "The ring was custom-designed and engraved, and the jeweler wouldn't take it back. My only hope is to find another girl named Jeannine, and with my luck, even if I do, she won't spell it the same way."

Fred learned an expensive lesson. We all have to learn lessons like that, and we hope that our own teens will learn them a little more cheaply. But here, as elsewhere, the great instiller of wisdom and discretion is a budget. Your teen can't spend more than he has. And if he knows where any given expense fits into a larger picture, he's going to make decisions that are much more responsible.

Peer-Pressure Problem #3: Lending, Keeping Track, and Repaying (or Not)

Just as teens can be overly generous with gifts for their girlfriends and boyfriends, they can also put their loyalty to their friends above sound financial judgment. Many good friendships have been ruined when one friend borrowed from the other, and your teen may need to learn this lesson the hard way.

CYNTHIA

"THEIR WHOLE FRIENDSHIP IS IN JEOPARDY."

Cynthia is the mother of a teenage daughter who finds herself in the middle of a dispute about borrowing between friends.

"My daughter Julia and her best friend, Taylor, are both 18, just started community college, and have gotten their first apartment together. I've known Taylor all her life, and she's like a second daughter to me, so when they have problems with each other—like now—I hear it from both sides. Right now, Taylor is kind of ticked at Julia over $11 that she lent her, and Julia won't pay back. I don't know why they're singling out this $11 to argue about, because they basically have no system of accounting for money and expenses. Julia pays for a lot of stuff for Taylor, which should make it a wash, but Taylor doesn't actually see it that way.

"Taylor loaned Julia cash at a store to buy something or other, but she isn't counting the times that Julia has paid for stuff at the grocery store for her.

"When Julia was complaining to me about it, I told her she needed to talk to Taylor about the things they buy—but it isn't quite that simple. Julia works at a supermarket, so she picks up steaks and stuff for dinner, and Julia pays, but Taylor works at a sub shop, so she gets sandwiches for free and brings them home. Taylor thinks that counts, because she works for them, but Julia doesn't, because Taylor doesn't pay cash for them.

"They both sort of think that food doesn't count, except that now Julia's thinking that she pays more for food than Taylor does, so she shouldn't have to pay back the $11, and Taylor thinks that if it's not food, it's borrowed money, and Julia should pay it back. Now they're barely talking to each other at all, except through me, and their whole friendship is in jeopardy over $11."

Both girls expected Cynthia to step in and solve the problem, but Cynthia prudently stayed out of it (remember the wise rabbi: "Does it matter profoundly?"). Teens have their own social rituals, and borrowing and lending are part of the sometimes convoluted world of teendom.

The problem with Julia's and Taylor's situation is that they have no concept of what money means and how it functions, and so it takes on a fuzzy symbolic meaning for them, with emotional overtones. Eventually, Taylor and Julia will forget the $11, but the problem won't go away. And eventually, it could very well explode on the two of them, destroying their friendship.

What do teens need to know about borrowing and lending?

Your teen needs to know that money is the simplest, clearest, most baggage-free form of communication—if you allow it to be. He needs to know that the responsibility for keeping it clean and simple is his. If he takes that responsibility, then he's in control of the situation. He has a voice in it.

That means make it clear and make it simple. If a friend asks to borrow a substantial sum of money—say, $25 or more—your teen needs to keep a record of it in writing. (See the example below.)

Make two copies: one for Jon, one for Alex. Each takes his own copy home and puts it in a desk drawer, and the matter is closed.

What if Alex doesn't pay the money back?

It can happen. And if does, Jon has to chalk it up to experience. Remember this lesson . . .

NEVER LOAN MORE THAN YOU CAN AFFORD TO LOSE

. . . and never lend Alex any more money.

Jon's Loan to Alex

Date: Jan. 27, 2003

Amount: $30

Repayment Due: Feb. 28, 2003

Signed: _____

Signed: _____

The chances are that it won't come up again. Alex will know, as well as Jon, that there's an outstanding unpaid debt. If Alex does ask to borrow again, all Jon has to say is "I don't want to go down that road," and his friend will understand what he means.

Teens give friendship unconditionally when they give it— their loyalty is one of their really good qualities. But this also means that they can be manipulated. In situations involving borrowing and lending, make sure your teen understands that he has to feel good about it. If he feels as if he's being manipulated, then it's okay for him to say no. It's okay to step back from the situation.

By the same token, you want to be sure that he doesn't feel *too* good about it. You don't want him to be getting his self-esteem from the fact that people owe him. Money and self-esteem should never be linked.

And what should Taylor have done about Julia and the $11?

Probably, in the first place, just what she did do. Eleven dollars isn't enough to require getting a receipt and filling out an IOU with a payment schedule.

As for not getting the money paid back, Taylor should just chalk it up to experience. Eleven dollars isn't worth losing a friendship over either.

But she shouldn't let it happen again. Roommates need to have a carefully negotiated agreement on separate and shared spending, and that's the subject of a later chapter. Meanwhile, next time Julia asks to borrow $11, Taylor can just say, "I don't want to go down that road again."

Peer-Pressure Problem #4: Borrowing

If your teen is the borrower, make sure he pays back what he borrows. Make sure he understands that it's a matter of honor and self-respect. If he has a friend who's the "rich kid" and expects to "lend" small sums of money that will never be paid back, make sure that your teen understands why he shouldn't get sucked into that kind of unequal relationship.

What if your teen is borrowing a lot?

You need to know, at least in general terms, what your teen's cash-flow situation is. If he suddenly has an expensive new skateboard that can't be accounted for within the scope of his income or gifts from relatives (make sure Grandma and Grandpa keep you informed on what they're giving your kids), then the money came from somewhere.

Dealing drugs? You always worry about something like that, but it may be more innocent. He may have borrowed it from a more affluent friend.

This is a situation where you must step in. You don't want your teen owing that kind of money, and you don't want him getting into that kind of habit.

I recommend getting other parents involved here. Call the friend's parents and make sure that this pattern isn't repeated.

Then I recommend taking the other kid out of the equation. You assume the loan. Pay the other kid yourself and set up a strict payment schedule with your teen to pay you back. Divide the weekly payment between his medium-term savings (that's not earmarked for his college fund) and his quick cash so that he feels some part of the pinch of it every week. It'll help remind him not to do it again.

Peer-Pressure Problem #5: Sharing

No doubt you've always taught your kids that sharing is a good thing, but when it comes to splitting the expense of an item with a friend, it's best to remind your teen to think through the consequences.

JOSH

Going Halves

When Josh started college, he and his girlfriend decided to "go halves" on a mailbox in the town where their college was located. Why, given that a mailbox rents for $20 a year? The only answer is teen logic, and sometimes teen logic can come back and bite you.

It came back and bit Josh. At the end of the semester, he transferred to another college, but when he went to get his mail forwarded, he was told that he couldn't. The mail would be forwarded for all users of the box—or for none. He could ask his girlfriend to forward all of his stuff, but frankly, he doesn't expect the relationship to withstand the separation, and he doesn't expect her to be much inclined to forward his mail.

If your teen shares an expense with another kid for something—anything—he may end up getting more than he bargained for.

Peer-Pressure Problem #6: The Rich-Kid Syndrome

Your family doesn't have to be rich in order for your teen to get caught up in the rich-kid syndrome. She just has to be perceived by her friends as a little more well off—the kid who's expected to pick up the check when they all go out for pizza, or to pay everyone's way into a dance club.

If your teen is the "rich kid" in her crowd, she may feel taken advantage of—or she may kind of like it because it may make her feel important. Either way, it's an unhealthy situation.

Talk to your teen about her feelings—what she feels that she has to do, and whether she knows how to say no. Help her develop strategies to keep from being put in the situation. Does she encourage it, perhaps even without meaning to, by suggesting that the gang all go somewhere that they won't really be able to afford?

Or is she on the receiving end? Is there a friend or two in her gang who always seems to think it's a great idea that they all go to the roller rink whenever she's around?

In that case, tell her that it's all right to say, "No, let's do something that we can all afford."

Suggest to her that she carry less cash when she goes out. If she has only $10 in her wallet, she won't be able to pick up the tab at the pizza shop.

The Jar System: A Quick Answer to the Problems of Peer Pressure

In my book *Money Doesn't Grow on Trees*, I recommended starting even young children on a Jar System to help them learn about basic financial responsibility. If you haven't been doing that and your child is now a teen, there's still no reason that you can't start. In fact, it can even get your teen out of a jam when she's feeling particularly pressured by her friends to buy that new CD, concert tickets, or the latest sneakers that she can't afford. She can simply say, "My mom set up this new system about money. I have to put part of everything I get into long-term savings for college, and part into intermediate savings, so I have only 10 bucks to spend on myself every week."

In later chapters, you'll be learning how to introduce your teen to the intricacies of setting up a checking account, getting her first credit card, and understanding investments. But when your teen is in a crowd of her spend-happy friends, sometimes a simple answer works best. How does the system work?

First, provide your teen with three or four clear jars, such as Mason jars. What goes into them? All the money your teen acquires, by doing work-for-money jobs around the house (younger teens) or summer jobs (older teens), or receives as gifts from relatives.

In its simplest form, the money is divided evenly into three jars. The first is labeled "Quick Cash"—spending money for that week. Your teen can spend it on anything she wants that's household-approved (if you have rules about candy or violent toys or even something like keeping kosher, those rules apply even if the kid is spending her own money).

The second is "Medium-Term Savings," for items your teen can't buy with one week's funds. This teaches planning, saving, and deferred gratification.

The third is labeled "Long-Term Savings"—your child's contribution to her college fund.

I recommend a fourth jar, the "Tithing Jar." I believe it's important that children learn that no one is an island, that we live in a larger world, and that we have a responsibility to be good citizens in it. So I recommend that 10 percent be put in this jar before the rest of the money is divided up.

7

TIPPING: WHEN, WHY, AND HOW MUCH

As instances of financial ignorance go, this one doesn't have the potential for devastation that some others do. It can, however, cause bad feelings or embarrassment, so it's a skill that must be learned.

A lot of teenagers don't know how to tip, unless they've worked in some branch of the service industry themselves. They don't realize that they have to tip at all, or if they do—and this can even be worse—they tip inappropriately. Sometimes this can be tipping too much, trying to show off. More often, it's tipping inadequately, out of complete ignorance of what the process is all about. A service worker may grumble privately when a teen leaves no tip at all for service, or she may politely explain to the teen how tipping works and why he should do it. But there are very few things that make that worker angrier than having the same teen give her $10 for a $9.75 cab ride and say, "Keep the change."

Tipping is part of functioning in the real world. It's one of the expenses we need to figure into our budgets, and it's one of the financial transactions that connect us, like so many little individual threads, to the greater society that we live in and that our kids will be entering.

The Tipping Quiz

Try this quiz on your teenager. Some questions may have more than one right answer.

1. Tipping is:

   a. An outmoded custom that goes back to the days before child labor laws.

   b. Part of the basic income of people in service industries.

   c. A reward for especially good service.

   d. Only expected of adults.

2. In a restaurant, you should tip:

   a. $5.

   b. 15 percent.

   c. Anywhere from zero to 25 percent—it depends on the service.

   d. Tipping is just picking your pocket—you don't have to do it.

3. In an airport, you should tip:

   a. The flight attendant.

   b. The curbside check-in attendant.

   c. The baggage claim attendant.

   d. Airport security.

4. Overtipping:

   a. Can get the person you've tipped in trouble with the IRS.

   b. Shows that you're a swell guy.

   c. Can create an awkward situation for all parties.

   d. Is always welcome.

5. If you and your friends hang out for a long time in a restaurant over a cup of coffee and dessert, you should:

   a. Tip 15 percent of the check.

   b. Leave a little more—you've taken up time that your server could have been waiting on another customer.

   c. Leave a little less—you've given your server a chance to take a break.

   d. I never tip anyway—why should this be any different?

6. You're on a school senior trip to Washington, D.C. . . .

   a. Carry a walletful of singles—travel involves a lot of tipping.

   b. Let the school chaperones handle the tipping.

   c. Don't carry any money all—big cities are dangerous. That's why no one expects kids to tip on a school trip.

   d. This is a trick question. Washington, D.C., is not a state, so rules on tipping don't apply.

7. All of the following people come to your house. Whom do you tip?

   a. The pizza guy.

   b. The UPS driver.

   c. The newspaper deliverer.

   d. The cable guy.

   e. All of the above.

   f. None of the above.

8. What do you do if you figured your finances wrong and don't have enough for a tip?

   a. Just don't leave one.

   b. Complain about the service.

   c. Explain your predicament to the server and apologize.

   d. Ask for the server's name and drop back the next day to leave the tip.

9. You're out with friends at a restaurant. You leave a tip based on your part of the check, but they don't. What do you do?

   a. Remind your friends that tipping is important.

   b. If they tell you that they never leave tips, make up the difference yourself.

   c. Just let it go—it's no business of yours.

   d. If they tell you they don't have the money, tell them that you'll cover it this time because the server deserves it, but if they expect to hang out with you, they'll remember to budget in tipping money.

   e. All, none, or some of the above.

Answers

   1. The right answer is *b.* As for the others, *a* makes no sense at all. But some teens think that anything they don't want to deal with must be some relic from the distant past, so this may fool a few.

   If your teen chose *c,* it's not a wrong answer, by any means. But for a teen who's still learning to navigate in an adult financial world, making judgments about the quality of service is probably too much to ask and may encourage snobbery and judgmentalism on the part of the teen. There may be exceptions for incredibly bad

Restaurant Tipping

How much do Americans actually give for satisfactory service?

0–5% tip	10%
6–10% tip	18%
11–15% tip	35%
16–20% tip	26%
More than 20%	6%
Don't know	5%

Source: The Associated Press, 2002

service, but your teen may not know enough to take into account, for example, the possibility that because a couple of workers didn't show up, your server is covering the whole floor by herself. Kids don't need to be making these decisions.

As for *d*, my comment is just the opposite. Kids *do* need to participate in the adult world on this level. A server, a cab driver, the doorperson who gets you the cab—each one does just as much work for a teenager as he does for an adult, and his time is worth just as much. The world doesn't owe your teenager a living.

2. A tempting answer is *c*, but the correct one is *b*. It's best to stick with the 15 percent rule. As we've already discussed, teens aren't yet savvy enough to make these types of decisions.

It's important that your teen understands why *d* is a totally unacceptable option. In service professions, tips are an integral part of an individual's income. People working in these professions are paid less in salary, with the understanding that tips will make up the rest. If they were paid the whole thing in salary, the cost for the goods and services you're getting would be a lot higher.

Furthermore, they're paying taxes on those tips, whether you give them or not. The IRS figures estimated tips into the income of a service employee.

3. Both *c* and *d* are dangerous answers. A tip to those folks could be—and should be, in these days of heightened airline security—construed as a bribe. Flight attendants don't get tipped, but the guys who handle curbside check-ins do. If your teen doesn't get this one—if you didn't get this one—it's understandable, or at least it is to me, and I'm a frequent traveler. And a sophisticated one, I always thought. But recently, on a flight out of Atlanta, I saw the woman in front of me handing a bill to the curbside check-in guy, so I asked him: "Is it customary to tip you?"

"Yes, ma'am," he replied. "Our hourly pay rate is based on the idea that we'll get tips."

"I never knew that," I said.

He sighed. "Lots of people don't."

A dollar a bag is the right tip at the airport check-in. What you have to remember is that this guy is fulfilling the function of a porter or baggage handler, whom you would naturally expect to tip.

4. The correct answer is *c*. It's not appropriate for a teenager to play the role of the last of the big spenders. It's okay for Frank Sinatra to throw a C-note to a hat-check girl at the Sands or the Stork Club, but leave that kind of behavior to Frank and the Rat Pack. For a teen to do it smacks of showing off.

And there are instances when it may be appropriate for an adult to give a gratuity, but totally inappropriate for a teen, such as slipping something extra to the maître d' in a posh restaurant to get a better table.

Teens are still apprentice adults, and they still have to accept the place of any apprentice in the pecking order, which means, in this case, that there are some ways that two adults can act with each other, but it's inappropriate behavior when the situation involves a teen and an adult.

If an adult gives a tip to the maître d' for a better table, it's probably because she has an ongoing relationship with the maître d'—she comes to the restaurant regularly and is an especially valued customer. Or it's a power perk—a visiting Texas oilman can try it, but it may not work even for him.

A teen who tries it—and this is the point—comes off looking like a naïve rube, which is humiliating but not the end of the world, or a snotty rich kid, which really is bad.

5. There are two reasons for giving this quiz to your teenager. The first is, of course, to find out just how much she knows about tipping.

The second is to pay attention to the answers. If your teen answered, "I never tip anyway—why should this be any different?" or even "Leave a little less—you've given your server a chance to take a break," start looking at some of the earlier answers. "Tipping is just picking your pocket . . . an outmoded custom . . . something that kids don't have to do . . ." or, later on, "Complain about the service" as a response to question 8—these answers suggest that you need to do a little more talking to him about personal responsibility and the way we live together in a humane and civilized society.

A is an acceptable answer, but a little insensitive; b is better. In this case, a reasonable amount over the standard 15 percent is not ostentatious; it's an acknowledgment of the value of someone else's time. And this is a good time to point out to your teen that money is not a replacement for other social graces. Ever. A tip doesn't ever take the place of politeness.

6. No, it's not a trick question, but d is definitely a trick answer. Just to see if your kids are paying attention. Of course you tip in Washington, D.C., the same as in any of the 50 states and Canada, Mexico, or any other foreign country. And of course you want your teen to be extra specially careful on her own in a big city. But the answer is a. The school isn't responsible for meals being served to your teen in the hotel coffee shop, bags being

brought to her room, cabs being called for her, or coffee stains being taken out of her best shirt. Travel time will be tip time in many, many ways (see below for more details), and as the traveler, your teen is responsible for being prepared.

Very important—this advice applies to older teens only. On any class trip for your junior-high-school-age kids, you should expect the chaperones to take care of all the tipping, and you should not expect your child to carry around extra cash.

It is appropriate, however, for junior-high-school-age kids to ask the teacher or chaperone, "Are there any places during this trip where I'll be expected to leave a tip?" This falls into the "there are no stupid questions" category. It's part of learning to be responsible.

7. If the cable guy is Jim Carrey, bar the door. Otherwise, it's not necessary to tip him. He's a professional getting a good hourly rate for what he does. Someone should be tipping the newspaper deliverer, but it's probably not your teen's responsibility. Most likely you or your husband ordered the delivery in the first place. Only one person in the household needs to take care of a tip or a Christmas gratuity for someone who performs a service for the household.

The answer is *a*. Your teen should tip the pizza delivery guy if she's the one getting the pizza—now it's a service being done for her.

Failing to leave a tip when it's called for is more than a faux pas; it's the next thing to stealing. It *is* stealing. It's theft of services.

Offering a tip when it's not called for is less serious, but it is a faux pas. It can even be regarded as an insult, though for the most part the person on the receiving end will take it as a forgivable blunder if a teenager does it. You don't tip a professional who receives good compensation for his work already. You don't tip the owner of a business (if you're not sure whether someone's the owner or not, either err on the side of caution and tip, or ask). You don't tip in any circumstance where a tip could be construed as a bribe—that is, in exchange for services you're not really entitled to.

8. If your teen chose *c,* that's not bad. Actually, most servers are a pretty understanding bunch, and they'll accept it. *D* is a better answer. There's something wonderful about *anyone* taking the extra step to do what's right, and it's especially wonderful if that person is a teenager.

9. The answer is *e,* sort of. That is to say, there's no cut-and-dried answer to this one. It's a good question for a family discussion, and a good way to open up a lot of issues regarding attitudes toward money.

The Delivery Charge
That Doesn't Pay for Delivery

Some professions seem to get more respect than others when it comes to tipping. And delivery guys—who frequently have to use their own cars and who are subject to robbery attempts second only to cab drivers—seem to have to struggle for recognition. The Web site tipthepizzaguy.com has undertaken a mini-crusade against pizza chains that have started to add a $1 "delivery charge."

Their argument is based on the premise that most people assume that a "delivery charge" means money in the pocket of the driver, which in fact it does not. If customers assume the driver is getting the surcharge, they aren't going to give a tip.

"Despite what it's called," according to tipthepizzaguy, "the delivery charge pays for general costs. The purpose is to offset the cost of food and overhead. This is a price increase in disguise. The driver does not reap a monetary benefit. There is no talk of it reaching the driver as wages remain stagnant."

Now that you and your teen have made it through the quiz, here are some general guidelines for teen tipping—when it's appropriate, when it's unnecessary, and how much is right. And by the way, don't forget to have your child figure tips into his travel/dining/entertainment budget and include them if he's keeping a No-Magic-Money Log (as described on page 46).

Eating Out

At a regular full-service restaurant, teach your teen to tip 15 percent. That's based on the total bill. Don't start worrying about whether or not you should tip on the tax, or subtract the tax before you figure the tip. It'll drive you nuts, and it's not worth it. Take the figure at the bottom of the check and figure the tip according to that.

Many restaurants will automatically add a 15 to 18 percent service charge to the bill of a large group, and that charge *is* the tip. It's taken care of; there's no need to add another 15 percent on top. This doesn't mean that the group can't leave another 5 percent on the table if the service has been really good.

Most restaurants don't have coatrooms anymore, but some traditional restaurants do, and a dollar for the coat-check person is appropriate.

Don't Make Them Pay
for Your Good Fortune . . .

The major exception to the figure-on-the-bottom-line rule: If the bill has been reduced by coupons or any other sort of free offer, figure the tip on what the meal would have cost at full price.

Restroom attendants, on the other hand, are making a comeback in many restaurants and nightclubs in cities. Some very posh places hire attendants as part of their full-time staff, giving them a salary and benefits. Most places, however, use a service that provides attendants, and these folks are quite often working for tips alone. A dollar is appropriate here; $2 is not inappropriate either. And remember, if anyone gets sick and someone has to clean up the mess, that someone is the restroom attendant. Under those circumstances, I'd tip $5.

It's not necessary to tip the host, hostess, or maître d'.

What about tipping at less-than-full-service restaurants?

In a fast-food place, or any other sort of counter-service place, there may be a tip jar on the counter. It's not necessary to leave a tip, but those kids aren't making any kind of a fortune back there. It doesn't have to be much—probably in the vicinity of 5 percent of the order, certainly not more than 10 percent. In this one case, since a tip isn't really demanded, there's nothing wrong with just dropping in whatever change is returned.

If it's a partial-service restaurant, however, where they put out a place setting, bring water, and bus the table, then 10 percent is definitely appropriate.

Food Delivery

This one's particularly important for teens, who do order in a lot. There are differences of opinion on this. Some suggest tipping as in a restaurant, 15 percent of the total bill. Others suggest a dollar amount, which will vary with two factors: how large the order is and how far the driver has to come; for example, $1 to $2 for short distances, $2 to $3 for longer distances, and $5 or more for large deliveries.

The dollar-amount theory makes a good deal of sense, because the transaction is going to be carried out standing up in a doorway, not sitting down at the table, and it will simply be faster and easier.

A Glimpse at the Other Side

The next time you're tempted to toss a few coins to the pizza delivery person and quickly shut the door, consider this confession from a delivery man:

"I deliver pizza part-time, and I keep a list of the good tippers and bad tippers. I love to be late on the bad tippers. 'Tips' means: To Insure Prompt Service. If they don't tip, they get it cold—real cold—then I try to lose them as customers. I always go to my good tippers first. That's law number one."

And easier is good. Remind your teen that the difference between an inadequate tip and a good tip is generally minuscule, and rounding 15 percent up to the nearest dollar, if it means spending an extra 30 cents, is not the same as trying to be Frank Sinatra and flipping a C-note to the hat-check girl.

Giving a larger tip for a longer trip makes a great deal of sense—the driver, in most cases, has to pay for his own gas.

Going Out

At a dance club, expect to tip the DJ a dollar to make a request, and since DJs take their work of keeping the dance floor filled very seriously, and the request may not quite fit the pattern, expect to wait awhile to listen.

Since dance clubs are frequently kid-oriented places, the rules about "showing off" are a little different. And if it's your teen's anniversary, and he wants to slip the DJ $10 to hear "our song" just as he gives his girlfriend that (not-too-extravagant) special gift . . . hey, it's probably not too extravagant a gesture for true love.

At a restaurant with a piano or piano-bass duo, there'll be a tip jar on the piano. For a request, $1 or $2 in the tip jar is appropriate. And if the music has been particularly enjoyable, there's nothing wrong with leaving a dollar even without having made a request.

How about street entertainers . . . that is, in places where they're legal? There's no rule here. But if it's enough to stop and listen to, why not show appreciation? This could be the next Kenny G or David Copperfield. Leave a dollar or a handful of change. For a really extraordinary talent—and they're out there—why not leave $5?

Generally speaking, ushers at sports events expect to be tipped (a dollar) for showing you to your seat and wiping it off; theater ushers do not. Why? I don't know. Just tradition.

On the Road

If a destination has valet parking, give $1 to $2 when picking up the car. Sometimes, if a driver—like a doctor, or a journalist covering a breaking story—thinks that she may need her car in a hurry, she'll tip the attendant when she leaves the car off and ask him to put it where it can be retrieved at a moment's notice.

It's inappropriate for a teenager to do this. Teens sometimes like to make this sort of gesture because they think it makes them look important, but the truth is it makes them look silly. If your teenager has a friend who's worked as a valet parking attendant, ask him what the attendants say in private about someone who tries to seem like a big shot.

For a cab ride, tip 15 percent of the meter, with a minimum of 50 cents, even for a really short trip.

For a limo driver, it's 15 percent of the total bill.

It's not necessary to tip a mechanic or a gas station attendant—most places have self-serve gas pumps anyway. Mechanics are professionals, well paid for what they do.

How about a towing service? Or a road call? This is a special service, and many people do tip for it—from $5 to $20 for someone who comes out to jump-start a car, change a tire, get into a locked vehicle, give a tow, and so forth. The amount to tip depends on how tough the job is and how far the person has to come.

What if it's a Good Samaritan—not someone sent out from a garage or a locksmith, but a nice guy who stops to help out?

It's appropriate to offer compensation. If he declines, however, then give him warm thanks, and don't embarrass him by pressing money on him.

What if your teen is the Samaritan, and the motorist he's helped wants to pay him something for it? It's up to the individual, but my advice is, in general, don't take it. That's not why people help other people. But I can't walk in someone else's shoes. If your teen really needs the money, and the help was substantial, and the offer is sincere . . . it's up to the individual. Many people really get satisfaction out of giving a token of appreciation to a young person who's helped restore their faith in the goodness of young people.

Further On down the Road

Younger teens traveling with their parents are not going to be responsible for tipping. When traveling with teens or preteens, it's a good idea to point out, discreetly, where you give a tip, because the more that kids understand about financial transactions in the world they're going to enter, the better.

Older teens may well be traveling by themselves—to see grandparents, even to visit friends who've moved to a different part of the country—so they need to know the etiquette of tipping in airports.

Teens traveling as a group, for a senior trip or other such event, will have some of their tipping situations handled by their chaperones, but they may be responsible for others. You should tell your teen to ask the chaperone at the beginning of the trip in which

What Does a Concierge Do, Exactly?

Here are some of the tip-worthy services a concierge may provide.

• Getting a dinner reservation or tickets to the theater, a sporting event, or a concert

• Arranging for car services

• Giving directions in an unfamiliar town

• Planning an entire day of activities

situations they'll be expected to tip and which will be taken care of by the chaperone for the group.

College-age teens may be on their own frequently in airports or hotels. So here are some of the major tipping situations your teen should start learning about.

At airports, the first person they're likely to meet is the shuttle driver, who takes them from long-term parking or the car-rental return (tipping isn't necessary at the car-rental agency). If the driver takes the bags out of the shuttle and puts them on the curb, tip him a dollar or two per bag.

We've discussed the curbside check-in attendant, who gets tipped at the same rate. Travel guides will also tell you about tipping skycaps for carrying your bags (same rate), but many people—including most teenagers—don't use skycaps, and there isn't any reason that they need to, what with wheels on bags these days. If your teen is planning foreign travel, a good bon voyage gift is a travel guide that includes information on tipping, because every country is different.

If your teen has special needs—she's in a wheelchair or on crutches—and she gets special assistance, she should tip $3 to $5.

The same rate is appropriate for a bellhop or luggage handler who takes care of bags at a hotel. If the bellhop takes the bags all the way to the room, your teen should tip $5.

Special services at a hotel require tips: room service (15 to 20 percent, as with waiters), a concierge (generally $5 for a more involved request). And don't forget the chambermaid. Your teen may never see her, but we all see the results of what she does, so leave $5 per night in the room for her.

Personal Services

Not everyone gets manicures, styling, coloring, aesthetician's services, but everyone gets haircuts, so let's start there. The barber/hairstylist generally gets 15 percent of the cost of the haircut (not under a dollar, even at a really cut-rate apprentice school). For a magician with the scissors, one so good that your teen wouldn't entrust her hair to anyone else's hands even if it were on fire, a tip should reflect that appreciation.

Same goes for the colorist. Figure a 15 to 20 percent tip, unless she makes your teen look like a Titian, in which case she's worth more. If, on the other hand, she makes her customers look like a Dali, it's probably a good idea to go somewhere else next time (although your teenager might actually prefer it).

The manicurist also gets 15 to 20 percent (again, it can be more for someone who does a job that's to scratch and claw for); a shampoo technician gets $1 to $2.

In a day spa, the 15 to 20 percent tip range is about right for everyone who provides a skilled service, such as massage therapists and aestheticians. Spa attendants aren't necessarily tipped, but for particularly good and attentive service, it's not inappropriate.

Teens have other possible personal services that you and I would be less likely to avail ourselves of. Tattoo artists should get 10 to 20 percent of the fee, depending on the artistic quality of the work; teens should expect to tip 10 percent for body piercing.

In Your Home

Christmas tipping is a tradition—the doorperson, the newspaper deliverer, and so forth. You need to let your teen know who gets tipped and who doesn't, because it's part of giving her an education in the full spectrum of real-world financial transactions. These won't be gratuities she's responsible for, however. One parent will take care of all these Christmas bonuses for the whole family.

Your teen has to understand the concept, not just because she'll be responsible for it all someday but also because she may have Christmas tipping responsibilities right now.

Sit down with her and discuss it. What personal services does she get on a regular basis? A hairstylist? Yes, if she goes to one regularly, $10 at Christmas. A personal trainer? The same. (But a sports team coach . . . no.)

8

CREDIT CARDS: THEY DO KNOW THEY HAVE TO PAY THE BILL . . . DON'T THEY?

This may be the most explosive of all the "what you don't know can hurt you" items. A credit card represents what every teen wants: an all-access pass to the mall—or that's what they think it is. And if they don't understand what a credit card really is and what it can do *to* them as well as for them, it can become a ticking bomb in their wallets, ready to go off with shattering repercussions to you as well as to them.

The Credit Epidemic

A 2001 survey by the Jump$tart Coalition for Personal Financial Literacy revealed that one out of three high school seniors uses

Average Credit Card Debt of College Students

Freshman	$1,533
Sophomore	$1,825
Junior	$2,705
Senior	$3,262

Source: 1999 study by Professor Robert D. Manning, Ph.D., Rochester Institute of Technology in New York

credit cards, and half of those teens have cards in their own names.

Seventy-eight percent of college students have credit cards, and the average balance is $2,800.

A study by Nellie Mae, an organization that focuses on providing education financing for undergraduate and graduate students and families, found that 1 out of 10 college students carries a balance of more than $7,800, and one-fifth of all college students have four or more credit cards.

A 1999 study by the Consumer Federation of America suggested that this figure may be way under the mark. Following are some of the highlights from this study, compiled by Robert D. Manning, Ph.D., a professor at the Rochester Institute of Technology in New York.

And They Keep Rolling In . . .

According to the Web site www.bankrate.com, the average college student gets 12 solicitations from credit card companies . . . per week!

- Twenty percent of students carry debts of more than $10,000.

- At some schools, college-loan debt averages more than $20,000 per graduating senior because of additional credit card debt, which was "refinanced" with student loans or with private debt-consolidation loans.

- The trend is toward starting into debt at a younger and younger age. In 1994, two-thirds of those college students who did have credit cards got their first card before college or during their freshman year. Just 4 years later, in 1998, that figure was 81 percent. In other words, although it's still true that not every high school or college student has a credit card, the ones who do have cards are getting them earlier.

Understand that I'm not saying that teenagers getting credit cards is a bad trend. I think that kids should be learning young how to handle credit. But it does mean that we have to become more vigilant about teaching our children good credit habits.

- Some students go so deeply into debt that they have to drop out of school and go to work full-time to pay it off. An Indiana University administrator estimated that they lose more students to credit card debt than to academic failure.

How Big a Problem?

"The unrestricted marketing of credit cards on college campuses is so aggressive that it now poses a greater threat than alcohol or sexually transmitted diseases."

—PROFESSOR ROBERT D. MANNING, PH.D.,
ROCHESTER INSTITUTE OF TECHNOLOGY

A Little Something for the Kids . . .

College credit-card marketers are an aggressive bunch, meeting incoming students with a smooth sales pitch and all kinds of cheap but attractive premiums like caps and tote bags. If you want to have a little fun, eavesdrop on College Credit Card Corporation, the "largest marketer of credit cards to college students in the United States," marketing *themselves* to credit card companies, at www.cdicccc.com/aboutcccc.htm:

"Well-trained College Credit Card Corporation representatives staff acquisition booths at targeted, high-traffic locations. Students are introduced to featured offers through a professional presentation. . . . Our representatives implement booth events in student unions, classroom buildings, cafeterias, and other high-traffic campus locations. College Credit Card Corporation also offers college 'take-one' poster distribution."

- Students with high credit-card debts are having trouble getting good jobs because employers are reviewing credit reports. In fact, most financial institutions won't even consider offering a job to a young applicant with a bad credit record. Their theory is, how are these potential employees going to handle someone else's money if they can't handle their own?

Credit card companies do market aggressively to young people, especially college students; there's no question about that. They have booths on college campuses, offering their products along with come-ons—premiums like T-shirts, beach towels, hats, and gym bags.

But the truth is, that's their business. Credit cards, responsibly used, are a cornerstone of the American economy and a benefit to the individual user. Misused, they can be a disaster. But teaching our teens the difference between responsible and irresponsible credit card use is our responsibility—not the credit card company's.

Unless you're planning to give your kids bus tickets and say, "See you in 4 years," you'll be in close touch with them while they're away at school. You will, in all likelihood, be taking them to their colleges and helping them get set up in their dorm rooms. So you can discuss the credit card companies and their blandishments as you pass them by—and it should be part of a discussion you've been having all along.

There's another form of card that's peculiar to college campuses—the "college money" card, which is a stored-value card intended for use at the college cafeteria and bookstore. It's a good idea to remind your college student that this is like the clothing allowance you may have given her in high school. It's meant to last for the whole semester, and once she spends it, it's gone, and there won't be any more till next semester.

This is important, because although the "college money" card may seem cut-and-dried—meals and books only—it really can be used for a lot more that's nonessential—college bookstores, especially, can be a treasure trove of apparel, gifts, junk food, and expensive toys.

The Credit Card Quiz

How much do your teens know about credit cards? Give them this quiz, for a start.

1. A credit card is:

   a. A way to buy more than I could buy without the card.

   b. An informal agreement to pay money owed.

   c. A way to get my parents to pay for things.

   d. A contract to pay, at a specified interest rate, for products and services bought using it.

2. If I get a credit card in the mail, it means:

   a. The credit card company has done a background check on me and determined that I can afford to pay for what I charge.

   b. I'm on a mailing list they've acquired.

   c. Since I didn't order it, I'm not responsible for charges I make on it.

   d. Big Brother is watching me.

3. Paying the minimum on a credit card is:

   a. The smartest way to handle payments—I can buy a lot and pay just a little.

   b. The amount that the credit card company thinks I can afford.

   c. The most expensive way of buying anything.

   d. A way of lowering interest payments.

4. I need a credit card because:

   a. I can use it as a legal ID anywhere in the world.

   b. I'll never be able to afford the stuff I want without it.

   c. Certain transactions, like online purchases or buying tickets to an event in another city, require it.

   d. All my friends have one.

5. If I get a credit card in the mail, I should:

   a. Keep it—you never know when it'll come in handy.

   b. Charge it to the max—that way they'll send me another.

   c. Decline it—it could hurt my credit rating.

   d. Use it to break into locked rooms.

6. Using a credit card to order online is:

   a. An invitation to disaster.

   b. Probably okay, but I wouldn't chance it.

   c. If you're buying from a reputable company, almost as safe as using it in a store.

   d. If you're buying from a reputable company, safer than using it in a store.

7. Online businesses are:

   a. Put through a screening process to make sure they're legitimate.

   b. All in trouble because of the dotcom bust.

   c. Like any other businesses—some ethical, some unethical.

   d. Exempt from regulation.

8. If my credit card is stolen:

   a. I'm screwed.

   b. No worries—the credit card company picks up the tab for anything the thief charges on it.

   c. I'm liable for $50.

   d. My identity has been stolen.

9. If I give out my credit number for identification purposes:

   a. I might win something.

   b. I'm asking for trouble.

c. I'm protected—no one can use it unless I give specific authorization.

d. I need to be careful not to get the number wrong.

10. If I get a bad credit rating:

a. It doesn't really count, because I'm still a kid.

b. It'll only affect me if I apply for another credit card.

c. It's sealed by the government unless I authorize someone to see it.

d. It can affect any financial transaction I enter into in the future.

11. A really smart way to get the most out of your money is to:

a. Get a cash advance on your credit card and invest it in the stock market.

b. Pay off your outstanding credit card balance as quickly as you can.

c. Keep paying the minimum on your credit card balance, so you can keep your cash free for other opportunities.

d. Keep your cash in a closet, and use your credit card as a paperweight to hold it down.

12. I can get a credit card in my own name at:

a. Age 16, but my parents have to pay the bills.

b. Age 18, but my parents are liable for the bills.

c. Age 18, and I'm legally responsible for my own bills.

d. Any age.

13. If I go over the limit on my credit card:

a. It's the card company's fault, so I'm not responsible for anything over the limit.

b. The store will decline my purchase.

c. A stern-faced manager will come out with a giant pair of scissors and cut my credit card into little pieces.

d. The card company will cover the cost of my purchase, bill me for it, and add on a substantial penalty for being over the limit.

14. My dad gives me his credit card to get a pair of $50 sneakers for school.

a. I really want a pair of $100 sneakers, so I'll just get them instead. It's only a credit card, so it won't really make any difference.

b. I'll get the $50 sneakers, but if I copy the number off the credit card, I can use it later to order some stuff online that I really want.

c. He said spend $50 on sneakers. He didn't say what I could or couldn't spend on a warmup jacket, sweatpants, shorts, a few T-shirts . . . and, hey, I'm going to need all that stuff, too. He wouldn't have given me the credit card if he didn't expect me to use it.

d. It's Dad's credit card, which means it's Dad's money. If I do anything more than buy the sneakers he authorized me to buy, it's stealing.

Answers

1. The right answer, of course, is *d,* but a surprising 52 percent of teenagers surveyed recently thought that it was *b,* "an informal agreement to pay money owed." Frankly, I find this hard to imagine, but it's true. There must be a lot of teenagers out there who think the world is a much warmer, fuzzier place than it really is.

If your teen answers *a* or *c,* it's time for a talk. Many people do think that a credit card is a way to buy more than they could without the card, and this is exactly the way that people get into serious credit trouble.

And, unfortunately, the major credit card companies count on parents to bail out their kids, which is why there are so many credit card company representatives on college campuses, eager to sign up college students. It's not because they think the students, all by themselves, are such great credit risks.

I say this because it's true. That is the card companies' philosophy, which is why it's easier for college kids than for recent college graduates to get credit cards. And I don't say it to single out the companies for blame. We all take a piece of that blame—parents, educators, and kids themselves—if kids are uninformed and irresponsible and go hog-wild with credit cards.

Teenagers—high-school-age and college-age kids—should have credit cards and should be learning to use them both at home and in school. One of my main concerns in recent years has been setting up financial literacy courses in both high schools and colleges.

There still aren't enough of these courses. It's the responsibility of the parents, but it's also the responsibility of schools, which ought to have the expertise to set up comprehensive programs.

A credit card, for a young person, is not a passport to consumer paradise. It's a tool for learning to handle money and developing a healthy credit rating.

2. Big Brother may be watching you, but a credit card all by itself is not enough to prove it. And credit card companies, when they send out those unsolicited cards, are taking no responsibility at all for your ability to use them responsibly. Nor are they giving you a gift—the minute you start to use a card, you enter into a contract to pay for what you buy. No, *b* may not be much of an answer, but getting a credit card in the mail doesn't mean much, except an invitation to spend more. It's not much of a commitment to your well-being on the part of the company. They just got your name off a list.

3. Boy, do you need to make sure that your teen knows that the right answer to this one is *c*. Too many people think that they're doing just fine if they keep paying the minimum. They may even think that they're somehow putting one over on the credit card company—but just the reverse is true. Paying the minimum means forking over a fortune in interest without making much of a dent on the principal. It means that you're compounding interest against yourself (see "How Long Will It Take You to Pay Off a Credit Card Bill?").

If your teen does use a credit card for a large purchase—furniture for a first apartment, for example—make sure that she has a clear plan for paying off the entire amount, with interest, within

How Long Will It Take You to Pay Off a Credit Card Bill?

If you only pay the monthly minimum, it'll take longer than you think to pay off your purchase. For example, if you charge $1,000 on a credit card that carries an 18 percent interest rate, and you pay the minimum payment of $25 each month, it will take you 153 months—or more than 12 years—to be rid of your debt. In that time, you'll have paid an astounding $1,115.41 in interest—more than your original purchase!

There are a few good Web sites that provide calculators you and your teen can use to figure this out for yourselves. Search keywords "credit card payment calculator," and you'll be directed to sites like www.bankrate.com.

Another Web site calculator, which you may want to check out if you want to be startled, shows you an estimate of the bank charges you paid for any given transaction: www.xe.com/ccc.

a certain time period—say, 6 months. If she can't do that, she needs to buy cheaper furniture.

4. The only good answer to this question—among those I've provided—is *c*. You don't need to keep up with the Joneses or buy more than you can afford (the best solution, if you want something you can't afford, is to save up for it). And a credit card can be a supplementary but not a primary source of identification.

Credit cards can also be a necessity in the modern world as a tool for dealing with emergencies, but this is true more for adults than for teens, who generally will—and should—turn to their parents in case of emergencies.

5. The correct answer is *c*. A credit card that you don't use can still damage your credit rating. If you have a drawerful of those unsolicited cards in case you need them for a rainy day, you're running your potential for accumulating debt up and up and up, even if you're not running up the debt. This can come back to bite you in the bottom in the circumstance, for example, of applying for a mortgage. The loan officer is likely to say, "I don't know about giving her this mortgage. She could turn around and charge $40,000 worth of stuff tomorrow."

Any teen who chooses *b* needs an intensive course in how money works. And if your teen chooses *d*, he's been watching too many private-eye movies.

6. Interestingly enough, the answer here is *d*. According to both Visa and MasterCard, "secure server" technology has reduced online fraud to a fraction of what it is in the offline world.

Remember, this only refers to entering a credit card number into a secure server. Your teen should never give his credit card number out over the phone—this is perhaps the most unsecure way of handling a credit card. You don't know who is on the other end of that line. In the past, some companies have hired convicts in prison to do that work.

And while we're on the subject, make sure your teen knows never to leave receipts or credit card statements where anyone else might find them and copy the number. When you go over a credit card statement with your teen, make sure to point out to him where the number is and show him how easy it could be to steal it.

7. Online businesses are like any other, so the correct answer is *c*. But 55 percent of teens mistakenly think that businesses must go through a screening process to determine if they are legitimate before they can put up a Web site.

8. Identity theft is a real problem these days, but it's far from a guaranteed consequence of losing a credit card. If your teen picked *d*, it may mean that he's being more trendy than thoughtful. *B* is wishful thinking, *a* is panicked thinking, and *c* is the correct answer.

9. If your teen doesn't know enough about how credit cards work, he's leaving himself open to fraud and deception. Giving someone your credit card number is like giving a stranger the key to your house and mentioning that you plan to be away for the weekend. Worse. The correct answer is *b*.

10. All of the first three answers represent different degrees of the same problem teenage thinking—that nothing will touch them, that they can still get away with all kinds of things. *D* is the only correct answer.

It's important for teens to understand very clearly that *c* is a wrong answer. A bad credit report is never going to be a secret.

There's a lot of misinformation floating around about bad credit ratings, all of it one version or another of "it's not so bad." But it's very bad. A bad credit report never leaves you. A lot of people—and not just teenagers—think that even if they declare bankruptcy, it'll be cleared from their record in 7 years. Well, it won't be. It stays on your credit report forever.

11. If your teen chooses *d*, that means she has a fear of the damage that unwise use of credit cards can cause, and that's better

than not having a healthy respect for the destructive power of credit cards—but it's not the answer either.

More dangerous wrong answers are *a* and *c*. It's an excellent idea for your teen to learn to invest, and I'll be addressing that in a later chapter. But one of the most important rules of investing in the stock market is: *Never use it as a get-rich-quick scheme.* Taking on the high-interest payments of a credit card cash advance and expecting that some slick day-trading investments will yield even higher returns is pretty much the equivalent of throwing money down a well.

And *c* produces the same damaging result. There isn't any opportunity that's going to make up for the compounded interest you're letting yourself in for by paying only the minimum.

If you have credit card debt, there is no greater return on your investment than paying down that debt and getting rid of those high-interest loans. So *b* is the answer.

12. C is correct. You can get a credit card in your own name at age 18, and you're legally responsible for your own debts. Legally responsible, sure—but are all 18-year-olds mature enough to take on that responsibility?

We all know that this isn't the case. So why don't credit card companies seem to know it? Why do 17-year-old kids get flooded with mail from credit card companies offering them extravagant lines of credit "regardless of your credit history and without any employment verification or security deposits," as an e-mail solicitation to my son Rhett recently promised? Because credit card companies count on two things. First, that kids will be irresponsible with their first cards and run up whopping bills.

Wait a second. Can that be right? Credit card companies want to get stuck with bills that kids can't pay?

Not a chance—because of the second thing these companies count on: softhearted parents to bail the kids out. And it generally works.

13. We all wish for something for nothing, and some of us, not just teens, translate those desires into wishful thinking and actually start to believe—as in *a*—that it's true.

It might be good for us if *c* were the right answer, but that happens more often in the movies than in real life, and it won't happen to someone who just makes a charge or two over her limit. The responsibility lies with the cardholder to use a credit card wisely, and that brings us to the other two choices.

As for them, your teen needs to be very sure he knows what the fine print on his contract says, which means he has to read the contract all the way through. Depending on your teen's particular contract, either *b* or *d* could be correct. His purchase might be declined—but then again, it might not. Depending on the contract, he may have authorized the company to let him have those extra charges and then to tack on an over-the-limit fee, which can be substantial.

14. Of course, the only right answer is *d*. If your teen chooses any of the other answers—or is silently thinking any of the other answers—you have a potentially serious problem.

Stealing is stealing, and that's a moral absolute, but it doesn't always feel that way. Some kids who wouldn't steal from anyone else can rationalize that it's okay to steal from their parents. This is, in a way, a kind of logical leap from the "nagging nine times" rule. If you know Mom will ultimately give in, why not just do it the easy way and eliminate all of that bothersome nagging?

If kids don't absolutely understand what a credit card is and how it works—and that it is a real transaction involving real money that has to be paid in real time—then they may be able to fudge this moral absolute in their minds. Make sure that your teen knows that the unauthorized use of a credit card is stealing—it's taking real money that doesn't belong to you.

Pay special attention to any wrong answers that your teen

gives here, because any misconceptions about credit cards are potential hazards. Make absolutely certain your teen knows:

- The only really responsible way to use a credit card is to pay off the entire balance each month. If you fall behind at all, make it your number one priority to catch up.

- Credit cards are not a way to get more stuff than you can afford. What is the way to get more stuff than you can afford? That's simple. There is no way.

Getting Off to a Good Start

Since the single most important thing a young person needs to know about credit card bills is that they have to be paid, and that there's no free money and no free stuff, start with some education on how this works, before you put any kind of credit card into the hands of your teenager.

I've talked many times about the importance of making bill paying a family project, to give kids a sense of how budgeting works and how money is distributed. This is particularly important in the case of credit card bills, because there's so much information to be gleaned from one of them.

For starters, go over the bill itself with your teen, or even your preteen. Show him all the information provided there and how to find it. Make sure he can find and identify the following key items:

- Account number, closing date, credit line, and available credit

- Account summary—the history of transactions for the month and the new balance

- Payment information

- Payment record

- Information about interest rates

- Payment coupon—should include all current payment information, plus an area to note any address changes or corrections

If you keep up on your credit card payments, this is a great lesson for your kids. If you've fallen behind or, worse yet, gotten into the habit of paying the minimum . . . well, there's nothing like knowing that you have to set a good example for your kids to make you shape up, is there?

Making Sure Things Don't Get out of Hand

Never stop having a dialogue with your kids about money; the more you make it part of your everyday life, the more they'll feel comfortable talking about it. You can discuss what they're buying, what they're spending, how closely they're staying on budget. The more you keep lines of communication open, the more they'll know that you aren't going to kill them for making a mistake.

Pay attention to what they have. If they're buying things they can't afford, taking trips that they ought not to be able to afford, where's the money coming from?

Watch out for this, just as you'd watch for signs of drug abuse. But money abuse is easier to spot, because the manifestations are generally so visible. If your teen has too much money, there are only so many reasons. It may be an illegal activity, like gambling or drug dealing. Or it may be credit card abuse. Either way, you have to find out. And don't waste time in doing it. The signs of spending too much money manifest themselves very quickly.

9

TEENS AND CARS: HOW *NOT* TO DRIVE YOURSELF CRAZY

We all want things that we can't afford, and we basically know that there are various ways to handle that problem.

- We can do without.

- We can save up.

- We can find ways to increase our income.

- We can buy now and pay later on some sort of installment plan that we can afford.

But what happens if we plan carefully in advance—save up, increase our income, or set up a plan to make payments we can afford—and suddenly we discover that we still can't afford it?

This is a situation that your teen may very easily find himself in when it's time to buy a car or pay his share of insurance on a family-owned vehicle. It comes from making his calculations based on too little information.

The Automobile Quiz

The quiz for your teenager on buying an auto is a short one.

1. What are all the different costs associated with buying a car? How much are they?

2. What are all the different costs associated with operating a car? How much are they?

If your teen left out any of the costs on either of these lists, he's in for a rude shock when he goes to buy a car—and an even ruder one after he's bought it.

The Cost of Buying a Car

Your teen has been stashing away money for months, and he finally has enough to go car shopping—or so he thinks. Waving the newspaper in front you, he says, "Hey, this ad says they have a 1997 Swoosher for $2,000! I've saved up $2,000, so I can go right down and buy it!"

But you know that he'll need more than the $2,000. He'll also need money for:

• Sales tax

• Registration fees

• An inspection

- The insurance premium

- Extras

The exact price tag on all these items? That's for your teen to research. They'll vary from state to state, and insurance quotes can vary quite a lot.

Before your teen goes car shopping, make sure that he has done this research and knows what all these figures are.

Also, your teen should know exactly what he's buying, which means making a list of desired features, and he needs to understand that the extras aren't guaranteed to be in every car. So if he wants a super-high-powered sound system, and the car won't be complete until he has it, make sure he knows that the Tooth Fairy won't bring the sound system and install it. He'll have to budget for that, too.

By the same token, he shouldn't be paying for a lot of extras that he doesn't need. If he's not going to be ferrying a 3-year-old around, he most likely won't need a videocassette player in the backseat.

Insurance

Insurance is the biggest of these expenses, and the most complicated. Your teen needs to know not only the cost of auto insurance but also what kinds of auto insurance are available, what each type costs, and what each one covers.

Your young driver should also know that the type of car she buys will make a difference in her premiums—the better the safety record, the lower the premiums. This means, among other things, if you're even thinking about letting your teenager buy an SUV . . . don't. Insurance premiums for these vehicles are right up at the top of the list, because (a) they're accident-prone (especially rollovers) and (b) they've been shown to encourage unsafe driving, especially among younger drivers.

Here's a list of different kinds of insurance coverage.

Liability insurance. This insurance helps protect you and your assets if you caused an injury to others or damaged the property of others with your vehicle and are determined to be liable. *Bodily injury liability* protects you in the event you are determined to be responsible for an accident in which someone was hurt or killed. *Property damage liability* covers the damage your vehicle has caused to someone else's property, such as their car, their mailbox, or a fence on their land.

Collision and comprehensive insurance. Collision coverage pays for damage to your own auto resulting from a collision with another vehicle or object, or from a vehicle rollover. Your car is covered no matter who caused the accident. Comprehensive coverage pays for damage to your auto caused by something other than a collision. This includes theft and vandalism as well as disasters such as fire, flood, and hail.

Medical payments coverage and personal injury protection insurance. Medical payments insurance covers the cost of doctors, hospitals, and funeral expenses for you and your passengers that result from an accident, regardless of who is at fault. This coverage will protect you when you drive another person's car (with permission) or if you or a family member, as a pedestrian, is struck by another vehicle. The availability of medical payments insurance varies by state.

Personal injury protection (PIP) is a form of no-fault insurance required in states with no-fault laws. This coverage is a broader form of medical payments insurance. It pays for medical care, lost wages, and replacement services for the injured party (for example, paying for a babysitter for children while a mother is hospitalized). It pays regardless of who is at fault in an accident.

Uninsured/underinsured motorist protection. If you are involved in an accident with an uninsured driver, you have very little chance of collecting payment for your damages from that driver. Uninsured motorist (UM) coverage pays the cost of damages and injuries resulting from being hit by an uninsured driver or by a hit-

and-run driver. Both you and your passengers are covered for medical expenses, lost wages, and other injury-related losses. You may also be able to collect for pain and suffering.

Similarly, underinsured motorist (UIM) coverage will pay for damages that exceed the amount of coverage carried by an underinsured driver. Both UM and UIM coverage are subject to policy limits. For some coverages, a deductible may apply.

Make sure your teen understands that insurance rates are based on a clean driving record.

Driving the Family Car

Adding a teenager to your insurance policy can more than double or triple your premiums. So your teen must understand that he has to pay the extra cost on the policy, *even if he doesn't buy a car of his own.* Driving is a privilege, and it's a privilege that comes with a price tag.

Before you add your teen to your policy, talk to your agent—with your teen present—about the possible consequences, in addition to the increase in your premiums. For example, in many states the company can cancel your policy after one accident, or even one moving violation, by a teenage driver.

Also, find out what you and your teen can do to reduce the cost of premiums. Again, these will vary from state to state and from carrier to carrier, but here are some things that will generally make a considerable difference.

- Have your teen take and pass a driver-training course.

- If your teen is a good student, make sure that his grade record is part of the package you present to your insurance agent. Many companies will give a break in premiums for good grades—not as a reward for studying, but because their actuarial tables show that good students get in fewer accidents.

- Put limitations on how much your teen drives the family car—and on what family car he's allowed to drive. Some insurance carriers will adjust the premium if your teen is driving only the older, cheaper car. Others will automatically assume that he's driving the new, expensive car and base the premium on that, so be careful. If there's a substantial difference here, you may want to shop for a new insurance carrier.

- Look into premium adjustments for the amount your teenager drives. If he's driving to school each day, that may make him look cool, but it also may add big bucks to your premiums. If you can list your teen as an "occasional driver," that will make a big difference in the amount of your premiums.

It's a good idea to make a very specific contract with your new driver that includes financial issues about operating a car, citizenship issues (like keeping good grades), and road-responsibility issues. Most insurance companies have some version or other of this form, and you can pick them up easily. My version of it is on page 148, covering not only the issues but also the consequences.

Go over this contract with your teen to make sure that he understands it. He needs to understand that his driving privileges depend on following it.

Some items to consider adding, or at least discussing with your teen, include the maximum number of teen passengers he's allowed to transport, the highest volume at which he can play his car stereo, his ability to change a flat tire, and clear instructions on what to do in case of an emergency.

Accidents

Your teenager needs to know the costs of even a simple fender bender, and she needs to understand that there are three different ways that having an accident costs you: repairs to the car, an increase in insurance rates, and a decrease in the resale value of the car.

More than in any other category I've discussed in this book, your teen needs to have a thorough understanding of all the consequences of careless driving—because they're so immediate and can be so devastating. So before she gets her license, plan to spend a good period of time really immersing her in all the ramifications of driving. And make as much of it as possible hands-on experience.

Some of that hands-on experience goes without saying. You'll take her out to a large, deserted space for her first lessons behind the wheel. You'll enroll her in driver's ed classes. You'll teach her about using turn signals, parallel parking, filling a gas tank, changing a tire, and reading all the gauges on the instrument panel (well, no one knows what the "check engine" light means).

But how are you going to give her hands-on experience in having an accident? The first rule of driving is to avoid having accidents.

True. But you can have her find out for herself about the cost of an accident.

Make it a research project for your teen.

Tracking-an-Accident Research Project

First, visit an auto-body repair shop and an auto mechanic's shop. Interview the owner or one of the workers. Ask them to show you the results of several collisions, and write up a report on each one of them based on what the mechanic tells you. Write up reports on at least three from the body shop and three from the mechanic (go to more than one shop for each, if necessary). Were the cars totaled? Could they be repaired? What does it take to make a car totaled, or not worth repairing? What happened to the occupants of the vehicle? Write up the results on a worksheet like the one on the opposite page, filling in the first three rows.

RESULTS OF AN ACCIDENT

List of Damages to the Car	
What Happened to the Occupants?	
Cost of Repair	
Insurance Deductible	
Impact on Insurance Policy Premiums	
Impact on Trade-In Value of Car	

Next, visit your family's insurance agent. Show him the accident research reports you've prepared. Ask him how much you would actually have to pay out of your pocket for each accident if it happened to you. This amount is known as the deductible. Then ask how much your insurance premiums would increase—or whether your policy would be canceled. Add this to your worksheet in rows four and five.

Finally, visit a car dealer and ask to speak with someone regarding trade-in valuation. Show the person you talk to your worksheet of accidents for which the car could be repaired, and ask the effects on the trade-in value of the car. How much less would it be worth now, when you went to trade it in? Write this amount in the sixth row.

Now look over your worksheet. The numbers in front of you are just the costs that you can actually estimate. A lawyer can tell you that the potential costs of a lawsuit resulting from an accident are astronomical.

Follow-Up

Your teen has been researching the economic impact of each accident. But while she's following that trail, she carries with her the second row of the chart—what happened to the occupants of the car. And that's not just the driver; that's all the occupants.

The final part of this exercise: Interview a medical professional and a police officer. Write up reports on the most important costs of an accident, the human costs.

And in the interview with the police officer, make sure your teen asks this question: What happens to you if you leave the scene of an accident without reporting it?

This can be a more complicated issue than it used to be, as I discovered recently in a scary and sobering lesson.

I was at a deserted intersection when another car ran a stop sign and sideswiped me. I pulled over to the side of the road. As I got out of my car, I saw a big, beefy man get out of the other vehicle. His face had road rage written all over it. He had tossed his suit jacket aside and was rolling up his sleeves.

I didn't know what to do. Every instinct, every learned response said, *Don't leave the scene of accident.* But I knew I couldn't stay there, alone, and deal with this maniac. I got back in my car, locked the doors, and drove off—fortunately, the car would still run.

The other driver got back in his car and followed me, trying to run me off the road.

I drove straight for the nearest town, about 3 miles away, and straight for the police station. When he saw where I was heading, he veered off.

I had his license number, and I reported the details of the accident to the police.

"What should I have done?" I asked. "I know you're not supposed to leave the scene of an accident."

"You did exactly the right thing," the officer told me.

So make sure your teenagers know this. Don't get out of your car on a deserted stretch of road if there's any possibility of danger. And do carry a cell phone with you at all times when driving. If I'd had one then—this was a couple of years ago, when they weren't quite as ubiquitous—I could have called 911 immediately.

Ongoing Auto Expenses

Look over your teen's answers to the automobile quiz on page 139. What's on his list of estimated expenses? When I ask the kids attending my workshops the same questions, their answers reveal just how little they understand. Here are a couple of examples.

STEPHAN, AGE 17

Stephan correctly included insurance as a cost of buying the vehicle but left it off his list of operating costs.

"What about insurance?" I asked.

"I've got that covered," Stephan answered with the lofty assurance of someone who knows he's caught his elders napping. "See—there it is."

(continued on page 150)

The Contract with a New Driver

I understand that driving is a privilege, not a right.
1. In return for being allowed to use the family car, I agree to . . .

A. Manage the following maintenance schedule.

• Get oil changed _____

• Check tire pressure _____

• Wash vehicle _____

• Wax vehicle _____

• Clean interior _____

(For each item above, determine how frequently this should be performed and who pays for it.)

B. Take on my share of the following financial responsibilities.

• Cost of vehicle _____

• Taxes and registration fees _____

• Fuel costs _____

• Monthly insurance costs _____

• Maintenance costs _____

• E-ZPass _____

(Figure out the amounts above on the basis of how much the new driver creates an added expense and specify what the teenager is responsible for.)

2. Whether driving my own car or the family car, I agree to be completely responsible for the following:

• I will keep a grade point average of _____ *(fill in)*. If I go below, I understand that the consequences are: _____

• I will wear a seat belt at all times while driving. If I neglect to do this, I understand that the consequences are: _____

• I will make sure all passengers wear seat belts while riding with me. If I neglect to do this, I understand that the consequences are: ＿＿＿＿＿＿＿

• I will obey a driving curfew of ＿＿ on school nights and ＿＿＿＿ on weekends *(fill in)*. If I break curfew, I understand that the consequences are:

＿＿＿＿＿＿＿＿＿＿＿＿＿＿＿＿＿＿＿＿＿＿＿

• I will let my parents know where I'm taking the car, and let them know if my plans change. I understand that the consequences for failing to do this are: ＿＿＿＿＿＿＿＿＿＿＿＿＿＿＿＿＿＿＿＿

• I will not let anyone else not approved by my parents drive the car under any circumstances. I understand that the consequences for letting someone unauthorized drive the car are: ＿＿＿＿＿＿＿＿

＿＿＿＿＿＿＿＿＿＿＿＿＿＿＿＿＿＿＿＿＿＿＿

• I understand that the consequences of being ticketed for nonmoving violations, such as having an expired inspection sticker, are: ＿＿＿＿＿＿＿

• I understand that the consequences of being ticketed for a moving violation are: ＿＿＿＿＿＿

• I understand that the consequences of being in an accident are: ＿＿＿＿＿＿＿＿＿＿＿＿＿

• I will never operate a vehicle while under the influence of alcohol or drugs. I understand that the consequences of doing this are: ＿＿＿＿＿＿＿

• I will never allow alcohol or drugs in my car, even if I'm not using them myself. I understand that the consequences of doing this are: ＿＿＿＿＿＿＿

Signed ＿＿＿＿＿＿＿＿＿＿ Signed ＿＿＿＿＿＿＿＿＿＿
        (teen)   (parent)

"But that's only your first year's insurance," I told Stephan.

His face crumpled. "You mean I've gotta pay it every year???"

JENNA, AGE 17

"I want to get a car that costs $8,000. I can put $2,000 down and get a loan for the rest if my dad co-signs for it. And I work hard and make my own money, so I know he will cosign. So that's $6,000 I'll owe. And if I pay $250 a month, I'll have it all paid off in 24 months, so I'll own it free and clear by the time I start college."

"What about interest?" I asked.

"Oh, I won't be borrowing from a bank," she said. "I'll get the loan straight from the auto company."

"They still charge you interest," I told her.

"They do? That's not fair!!!"

Your teen needs to figure insurance (every year), an inspection (every year in most states), gas, tolls (if your state has E-ZPass or some similar electronic toll-collection service, he can keep track of just how much this expense is), regularly scheduled maintenance, and wear and tear.

How is he supposed to figure wear and tear? He can take an average mileage figure that corporations use and multiply by the number of miles he expects to be driving. (He'll underestimate this, so it's a good idea for the two of you to sit down and figure it out.)

Better yet, have him do some real research on the particular car that he plans to buy. Various consumer organizations (such as Consumers Union, which publishes *Consumer Reports* magazine) publish reliability charts on the frequency and expense of repair for every make and model of car. This will not only give him a better sense of how much maintenance he has to budget for, it also will teach him to be an all-around better consumer.

Make sure your teen understands that while he'll have to go on paying for insurance every year, that doesn't mean he'll have to pay the same rate every year. A safe driving record—and simply getting older—can mean a reduction in rates.

It's a good idea to shop around—and not just once, when your teen gets his first car and first insurance policy. You should comparison shop every couple of years. Insurance companies are competitive, and insurance rates can vary widely. According to a report published in February 2003 at the MSN Web site:

> A study by Progressive Insurance in 1998 and 1999 showed 6-month auto insurance rates varied an average of $481 across the country. This means that the same driver could receive a quote of $1,256 for a 6-month auto insurance policy from one company and a quote of $775 for the identical policy from another company. Yet, another study conducted in late 1998 showed almost 60 percent of consumers surveyed had not contacted an insurance company or agent to ask about rate information in more than 2 years.

And once again—because I can't emphasize it too strongly—a good insurance premium depends on a good driving record.

10

TEENS AT WORK

If your teen is working—and he should be—the two factors you need to consider and monitor are how much he should work and what kind of job he should take.

Working Too Hard

One of the real dangers related to spending too much is working too hard. Teenagers can start running up those expenses—continuing expenses, like a car, or accumulating expenses, like credit card debt—and get drawn into a cycle of working too many hours to keep up their payments. We know how debilitating that can be, financially and emotionally. If you're just barely making your minimum payments, you're never going to catch up. And if a teen is working more and more hours at the kind of jobs that most high school students can manage, he'll never get out of that rat race and into a productive growth cycle.

We all know that every new generation that comes along is lazy, shiftless, and unwilling to do good, honest work, as we did when we were young. Older generations have been saying this since the Middle Ages (literally—a scholar friend showed me some medieval manuscripts that contained exactly the same complaints). Our parents said it about us as well. Today's working generation, however, puts in longer hours—and at more stressful jobs—than earlier generations could ever have imagined.

And today's teens work more than we realize. The U.S. Census Bureau estimates that by the time they've reached 17, two out of every five teenagers are working nearly 19 hours a week— and many experts believe that this figure is too low. Another study, in the *Journal of the American Medical Association,* found that nearly 20 percent of high school students are working more than 20 hours a week. And a 1995 study by the University of Michigan showed that 12 percent of high school senior boys and 7 percent of girls worked more than 31 hours a week.

Wait a second . . . isn't working good for teens? Doesn't it teach them responsibility and the meaning of a dollar? Haven't I advocated that by age 16 teens should be off allowance and working for their spending money?

Yes, absolutely. Work is good for teenagers in all those ways and more. According to a 1998 report by the National Research Council and the Institute of Medicine, 17- to 19-year-olds were less likely to drop out of school if they had worked the previous year. And there's a side benefit: Teens who work tend to watch less television.

But too much of a good thing can very quickly turn into a bad thing. Teens who work more than 20 hours a week, according to the same study, are more likely to cut class, get lower grades, and drop out of school. Kids who are making more money at ages 16 to 19 are very likely to have less education and make less money when they reach ages 28 to 31.

And teens who work more than 19 hours a week are also more likely to smoke, drink, and do drugs, surveys have found, says Jeylan Mortimer, Ph.D., a sociology professor at the University of Minnesota in Minneapolis and author of *Adolescents, Work, and Family.* Spending that much time in primarily adult workplaces, according to Dr. Mortimer, increases the likelihood that teens will pick up their older coworkers' habits, including drinking and smoking.

The pressures of too much work added to a full school load can also raise a teen's stress level, leading to the same results: poor grades, higher dropout rates, and the potential for substance abuse. Kids today are subject to incredibly high levels of stress as it is. If we can lead them away from making that situation worse, we should.

It makes a difference what kind of work teens do. Dr. Mortimer found that good working environments, jobs that carry responsibility and have a socially valuable component (including volunteer jobs), can be of real benefit to teens. They can even help teens deal better with problems at home. (For more information, see "Choosing a Good Job" on page 158.)

How Much Work Is Appropriate?

Sit down with your teen and help her figure out how many hours she can afford to allocate to working and how much she can earn in those hours. Then create a No-Magic-Time budget based on those realities.

You can't, beyond certain basics, dictate how she's going to spend her money (although you can insist that she save a portion of it, just as you did when she was younger). You can, however, put a lid on how much time she'll spend on making it—and you should. This, for example, is not the way to figure out how many hours to work: "I need $1,200 a month to pay for all the expenses I plan on having, so I'll have to work 30 hours a week at $10 an hour."

It's time for a serious lesson in "opportunity costs" here if too much time at a low-paying job is going to hurt your teen's chances at good grades in school and limit significant extracurricular activities that will lead to a better college and a big difference in income down the line.

Your teen's number one responsibility is school, and everything else needs to be built around that.

The appropriate question is not "How do I work enough

No-Magic-Time Chart

Have your teen fill in this chart with the number of hours per day he spends on each activity. By subtracting the total from 24, he can then determine a reasonable amount of time that he can devote to a part-time job.

Activity	Time Allotted (in hours)
Sleeping	
School	
Eating	
Homework	
Sports/activities/enrichment	
Household responsibilities	
"Time off"	

hours to make $1,200 a month?" but "How do I budget the income I can make from working a sensible, responsible schedule?"

I actually don't believe that it's a good idea for a teen to have an after-school job during the school year. A full-time summer job, however, is a good thing, as is work on weekends during the school year.

So base your No-Magic-Time Chart on the teen's primary responsibilities. And just as financial advisors tell you to pay yourself first while making up a money budget, bring a "Pay Your Primary Responsibilities First" philosophy to your time budget, along with that other classic of money budgeting, fixed and variable time allocations.

Here's what I mean.

Nobody gets enough sleep these days. It is, however, the foundation that our physical and mental health are built on, and teenagers really need their sleep—8½ to 9 hours a night, according to the nonprofit National Sleep Foundation. So make sure that sleep time is budgeted as a fixed time allocation.

School hours are set in stone as well. Your kids have to go to school; they can't start cutting classes, or days, because of the demands of a job. Time to eat three well-balanced meals a day is also a fixed time allocation.

Homework, extracurricular activities, and household responsibilities can be variable time allocations, but they have to be figured out realistically—you can't shortchange them.

"Time off" means time, just for the teen, that he doesn't have to account for. In the movie *Broadcast News*, Holly Hunter, playing perhaps the most organized person on the planet, scheduled 15 minutes every morning for a good cry. Nobody needs to be that organized, but everyone needs to know that he has a certain amount of time for taking a walk by the river, watching reruns of *Buffy* on TV (even if she's not giving financial lessons), or just sitting under a tree and reflecting on the day's events.

Is there time left for an after-school job? There may not be. You can't force more than 24 hours into a day.

You Are What You Learn

Income and employment statistics from the 1998 report of the Census Bureau of the U.S. Department of Commerce:

Degree Level	Annual Income	Unemployment
High school dropout	$20,110	7.1%
High school diploma	$28,307	4.0%
2-year associate's degree	$36,392	2.5%
Bachelor's degree	$50,056	1.8%

And the gap just continues to widen. In 1975, an average college graduate earned 57 percent more than an average high school grad. Today, it's 88 percent more.

All this advice holds true for both teenage girls and boys—and I've been alternating pronouns throughout this book in order to make that point clear—but here's a place where boys are especially vulnerable. A 2002 study of the Massachusetts school system reported that boys were 36 percent more likely than girls to drop out of school.

Boys are more likely to spend a lot of money on their cars. Plus, they're often more likely to get jobs—construction jobs, for example—at more than the minimum wage and be seduced away from going to college.

During the economic boom of the 1990s, this trend was starting to become so pronounced that college freshman boys were almost becoming an endangered species, and jokes about affirmative action programs for boys had a ring of truth to them. Even in the current economy, a disproportionate 60 percent of college degrees are being awarded to women.

Choosing a Good Job

A good job is one at which your teen is going to learn something of value. At these jobs, teens take responsibility, deal with the public in a way that's more than rote work, or learn something.

Often, some of the best jobs in terms of long-term value are the ones that pay the least—like nothing. I'm referring to volunteer jobs, of course. They frequently can involve a lot more responsibility and can give your teen a chance to really make a difference.

Kids who want to make this kind of positive impact on society deserve our support. Perhaps consider an allowance that's half of what he'd make at the sort of job he'd get if he hadn't made this commitment. Perhaps you could treat him to a movie. Or you could pick up the tab for him to go out on a date once a week. In fact, I'd argue that they deserve our support later in their life, too. If your college senior tells you, "I really don't want to be an investment banker after all. I want to get a master's degree in physical therapy and work with kids with cerebral palsy," and you can afford it, I'd say set up a trust fund to enhance his income. I'm not putting down investment bankers, whose work I admire (I used to be an investment banker), when I say that they are not intrinsically worth so much more than people who help kids with cerebral palsy.

Every Job Is Not *a Good Job*

We usually think of work as being good for our teens—but that's not always the case. Some jobs out there are dangerous, presenting more danger than teens should be exposed to.

According to the National Institute for Occupational Safety and Health, 73 teens under age 18 were killed on the job in 2000—and 29 of them were under age 16. An average of 231,000 teenagers under 18 are injured on the job each year (see "The Five Worst Teen Jobs").

The Five Worst Teen Jobs

Steer your kids away from the following occupations, ranked as the five worst by the National Consumers League.

1. Driving and delivery, including operating or repairing motorized equipment

2. Working alone in cash-based businesses and late-night work

3. Cooking with exposure to hot oil and grease, hot water and steam, and hot cooking surfaces

4. Doing construction and working at heights

5. Selling items door-to-door in traveling youth crews

Child-labor laws, in most states, do not apply to kids age 16 and over, but even child-labor laws vary from state to state. (Idaho, for example, "restricts" young teens to a maximum of 56 work hours a week—and, no, that's not a typo). And when kids are theoretically protected by the law, they are often inadequately trained for what they have to do, and laws are often sidestepped. You can't count on the government to make sure your kids are protected on the job, or assume that all employers are responsible and benevolent. You have to take it upon yourself to know what's going on.

Helping Your Child Choose Her First Job

You need to be involved, and aware, when your teen is getting her first job, but you mustn't be domineering to the extent that you take all the responsibility out of your kid's hands. Here's how I suggest you handle keeping yourself apprised of your teen's work situation.

Be involved. Make decisions with your teen about what kind of work she can handle. Discuss the pros and cons of various jobs she may be considering. For some teens, there's a social-status component to working: It's acceptable to work as a cashier in a gourmet market, but unacceptable to do the same job at the local convenience store. Without casting too many aspersions on teen pecking orders, make sure your teenager knows that social status isn't the only factor that enters into the decision-making process about a job.

Discuss the safety aspects of various jobs—not only in terms of the equipment involved but also in terms of the number of hours, location, kind of supervision, and start and end times of work.

Talk about the educational and career-training aspects of various jobs and how they'll look on future résumés.

Set limits. Use the No-Magic-Time Chart on page 155. Set limits on how many hours per week your teen can work and how many days he must keep free from work. If you want your teen to work summers and keep the school year free, make that clear.

Check it out. You don't want to embarrass your teen, or make him feel as though you're belittling his self-sufficiency, by imposing yourself between him and his supervisor or coworkers. But there are things that you need to know and that your teen should know, too. Make sure that your kid does some research on the company's safety record. Have him check out the company's safety-training procedures and equipment, and how they stack up against state and federal guidelines. Have him do a little research on safety laws, specifically as they apply to minors.

To whatever extent you can do it, without subjecting your teen to on-the-job humiliation ("Here's Mommy, to see that bossy-wossy is taking good care of little Jimmy"), get a first-person impression of your child's workplace.

My daughter Kyle recently took a job as a hostess at a restaurant and bar. She was only 18, but she could do the hostess duties, which didn't involve the handling and serving of liquor. She assured me that it was a nice place, and I was confident that it was, but, nevertheless, a few friends of mine and I went there for an early dinner the next week and a late dinner the week after. We were introduced to the owner, so that he knew who I was and that Kyle wasn't some waif off the street whose parents were totally disconnected from her life. Plus, we looked the place over and got a sense of the environment (it was, in fact, a nice place).

It's not difficult to arrive at that level of discreet involvement. If your teen is working at a lumberyard, buy some plywood and Sheetrock. Your den can probably stand a little redecorating anyway. If he's at a driving range, go out and hit a few buckets of balls.

Keep lines of communication open. Talk to your teen about work. Listen to the funny stories, the stories about job satisfaction or things she's learned on the job—and the problems. Listen carefully and ask questions when a discussion of problems starts. Are they just the normal gripes everyone has, or should you start to be concerned?

Listen to things they don't tell you. Read between the lines, and read those awkward pauses and silences. Ask questions and let your kids know that it's okay to talk. Sexual harassment, for example, may be too embarrassing for a teen to talk about without encouragement.

Pay attention. Are you noticing any changes in your kid? Is he starting to get stressed-out, overtired? If it's a school-year job, is it affecting his performance at school? Is he unable to give any time to extracurricular activities that may be of more value to him in the long run?

Encourage them to empower themselves. It's hard for a teen on a first job to ask for a raise. You can discuss with your teen when a raise is appropriate, rehearse these conversations with him, and let him know it's one of an employee's normal rights.

11

WHEN WHAT YOU DON'T KNOW
CAN HURT YOU EVEN MORE

The topics and situations discussed in the previous chapters are serious enough for you to probably think, "Whew. It can't possibly get any worse than that."

Guess what? It can.

Gambling

Does your college student suddenly have a lot of money (or debts) that he can't account for?

Gambling may be the culprit. It has always been a potential hazard for teenagers. Betting seems like fun. It generally involves small sums of money—at least at first—and it has the air of the forbidden without seeming really dangerous. It can get out of hand, though.

And with the advent of Internet gambling and the proliferation of credit cards in the hands of teenagers, the problem has gotten much worse. Anyone with a credit card can gamble online—even your young teenager, if he has access to one of your credit card numbers.

Gambling addiction has reached epidemic proportions among college-age kids. It's as much as five times more common in this age group than among adults, according to Christine Reilly, executive director of the Institute for Research on Pathological Gambling and Related Disorders in the Division on Addictions at Harvard Medical School. Calls to the Council on Compulsive Gambling of New Jersey by people in over their heads because of Internet gambling rose 1,000 percent between 2001 and 2002.

And the consequences can be more devastating than you'd think. Gambling addiction is more likely than any other form of addiction to lead to suicide, according to Sharon L. Mitchell, Ph.D., director of the counseling program at the University of Delaware, because the bottoming out is accompanied by such devastating financial loss.

Frighteningly, gambling addiction does not get the attention it deserves at most colleges. But it needs to be treated like any other addiction—handled by skilled and trained specialists.

Gambling Losses Become Credit Card Debt

The average gambling addict ages 18 to 25 loses $30,000 a year, most of it put on credit cards.

Source: The California Council on Problem Gambling

The symptoms of gambling addiction include mood swings and an erratic pattern of spending. Unexplained trips to places like Las Vegas and Atlantic City can be a tip-off, but college students are much more likely to gamble over the Internet or with a local bookie than to go to the big gambling resorts. According to a 1997 study by the Indiana Gambling Impact Study Commission, the most common forms of gambling by teens ages 18 to 20 were buying lottery tickets, playing cards for money, betting on games of personal skill, and sports wagering. This was before the Internet gambling explosion, but all of these are still threats today.

Gambling addicts are likely to steal money from family, roommates, or friends. Be suspicious of a sudden change in patterns of making and getting phone calls and a sudden increase in calls from strangers. Gambling addicts will often have changes in sleep patterns, too, including sleep deprivation.

Authorities in the field warn that innocent-seeming family events—like a family poker night, trips to the racetrack, or NCAA tournament pools—can create the illusion that gambling is a benign pastime. They also discourage having "casino nights" as teen fund-raisers and giving lottery tickets as gifts.

CHARLES

"EVERY QUARTER I COULD BEG OR BORROW, WIN, OR, YES, STEAL WENT INTO THE SLOTS."

After getting the wrong message about gambling when he was just 9 years old, Charles quickly developed an addiction that soon replaced his other interests and alienated him from his friends.

"I started having a gambling problem as a young teenager, getting into every neighborhood card or dice game I could find or starting my own. I lost a lot of friends who just weren't interested in shooting craps or pitching coins every time we got together. I made new friends who shared my 'interest.'

"I personally think that sending a kid away to boarding school is a bad idea for all kinds of reasons, but it's a terrible idea for a young gambling addict. You're always going to find a game going on at even the preppiest of prep schools, generally run by older kids who are more than willing to clean out the younger kids.

"I don't know why I started gambling, and I certainly don't blame my father, who was actually trying to show me how stupid it was. But here's what happened. When I was 9 years old, my family went on a cruise, and the cruise ship had slot machines. I asked my dad what they were, and he said they were just a dumb way to lose your money. 'Look at this,' he said. He put a quarter into the machine, pulled the lever, and to his horror hit the jackpot.

"Yep, I got the wrong message. For the rest of that cruise, every quarter I could beg or borrow, win, or, yes, steal went into the slots."

I can't emphasize strongly enough. This is an addiction problem, not a discipline problem. Your gambling-addicted teen needs to be treated by an experienced counselor—not sent to his room.

Identity Theft

Here's a simple quiz for your teen on identity theft. Choose *a* or *b*.

a. I don't have to worry about identity theft, because I'm just a kid. And who'd want my identity, anyway? I'm still finding it myself.

b. Everyone needs to worry about identity theft. Thieves don't care about your personality, just your credit cards, cell-phone accounts, ATM cards, and so forth.

Yep, a simple answer here. Make sure your teen knows it's *b*.

What Is Identity Theft?

Identity theft happens when a thief commandeers your identity for the purpose of making financial transactions that benefit him and hurt you.

It's a modern-day phenomenon, because today there are all kinds of electronic ways of being you. You're much more a number, or series of numbers, than your grandparents and even your parents were, and your kids are going to be even more of a series of numbers than you are. Instead of calling them Generation X, or Generation Y, they should be called Generation 123 4567 89XYZ.

Rather than taking your money—or even your credit cards—the thief steals information about you: your bank and credit card account numbers, your Social Security number, and your name, address, and phone number. Armed with keys to your identity, the thief can then acquire his own credit card in your name or open a bank account in your name and write bad checks on it.

Identity thieves can get information on you by simply stealing your wallet or by taking more devious routes, such as completing a change-of-address form to divert your mail to another location or posing as a prospective landlord or employer to get your credit records. They can even get information that you thought was confidential off the Internet.

And there's nothing that says a store clerk can't also be an identity thief or in cahoots with an identity thief.

You can take precautions to minimize the risk of identity theft—and you should—by guarding your wallet, putting a lock on your mailbox, and being careful of information that you give out over the Internet. You can also use password protection on all your accounts and tear up or shred any documents that have personal or financial information on them before you toss them out.

Even so, you must keep in mind that identity theft can happen not only to you but also to any family member. So you should make sure that everyone in your family knows how to deal with the possibility of it happening.

Here's a tip that's particularly applicable to teens, who are especially prone not to look a gift horse in the mouth: If your credit card bill doesn't show up in the mail one month, don't take it as gift from a benevolent providence. If the bill was just lost in the mail, you need to get it re-sent, because you're liable for it anyway—and for the late charges. But if it's been redirected to a different address, you *really* need to know about that right away.

Worst-Case Scenarios

I'm sorry to keep bringing you down about what can go wrong in your child's financial and personal life. The truth is, though, terrible things can happen to kids when financial irresponsibility leads to this sense of powerlessness and irremediable despair. Terrible things can happen to families when a teenager's financial irresponsibility translates into a sense of imperviousness—"Nothing really bad can happen to me"—and its corollary, "It's my life and it's no business of yours what I do with it."

Examples of how wrong that is can be found all too easily and all too close to home. These are all things that have happened to friends or acquaintances of mine or to friends of friends.

Out of Control

You've already read a number of stories in this book about the damage that can occur when teens naïvely believe that as minors, they're not responsible for their own actions. But the following story may be one of the most horrible—in terms of both the teenagers' negligence and the devastating impact their actions had on the entire family.

JANNA AND TED

From Party to Prosecution

Janna was a banker; Ted, a lawyer. They both had jobs that required frequent out-of-town trips, and they couldn't always schedule them so that one parent would be at home. When their kids, Micki and Jason, were younger, they had a nanny. At 17 and 16, however, they had outgrown those days and were furiously indignant when Grandma was called in to stay with them while their parents were away—furiously indignant enough that it finally got to be too difficult for Janna's mom to put up with them, so she begged off.

Eventually, there came a time when both parents were away on business at the same time. They let the kids stay alone, with the usual promises—no parties, no drugs, no booze—all of which the kids broke as soon as the parents were out the door. The kids had seen Tom Cruise in *Risky Business,* so they knew that you could get away with outrageous wild parties and fix everything by the time your parents got home.

Except it doesn't work that way in real life. The parents came home to find the house trashed, lamps broken, and the smell of liquor everywhere.

The kids were defiant. "It's none of your business what we do with our own lives!" they shouted. "We'll pay for the damages. It's no big deal."

Nothing the parents could say made any difference in Micki's and Jason's attitudes, and they all went to bed angry and frustrated. It was the next morning that things really got ugly, when two state police cars from the Bureau of Criminal Investigation pulled up in front of the house.

Upstairs, Micki and Jason whispered to each other—"Are we in trouble?" "Nah, how can we be? We're minors." "And we didn't do anything wrong. . . . It was all in our own house." "Yeah, they're just here to lecture us."

But the troopers weren't there for Micki and Jason. They were there for Janna and Ted, who were arrested and charged with gross negligence, serving liquor to minors, and reckless endangerment. Several of the kids who had left the party had been picked up for driving under the influence (DUI)—a couple for DUI without a driver's license—and one group had been in a serious accident. The troopers told Janna and Ted that they were lucky no one had been killed, or they could have been charged with criminally negligent homicide.

Janna and Ted spent the night in jail. A different car came for Micki and Jason. This one was from social services. They were taken away, made wards of the court, and put into foster care—it was 2 months before Janna and Ted could get them back.

The parents spent $100,000 on legal fees, which kept them out of prison. The prosecutor's office ultimately accepted a plea bargain in which both of them received probation. Their lawyer—Ted's lawyer—arranged it so his plea was to a misdemeanor charge so that he wouldn't be disbarred. Hers was to a felony.

But a felony conviction turned out to be just as serious in Janna's profession. She lost her job—and her career in the financial-services industry.

It was also the end of their marriage. Janna and Ted were divorced within the year.

When the criminal charges were settled, the civil lawsuits began. The parents of the girl who was injured in the accident sued for $5 million; the lawsuit was ultimately settled for half a million. Janna now works as a waitress and has her salary garnisheed to pay the settlement and her legal expenses. She lives in a small apartment with Micki, who also works as a waitress and is hoping to save enough money to go to community college in a few years.

Jason does construction work part-time and has a drinking problem. Janna doesn't know what else he's doing. She doesn't see much of him these days. But she fears the worst.

Drugs

One of a parent's worst nightmares is discovering that her teen is involved with drugs. Because even the thought of it is so scary, it's understandable that many parents naïvely fail to see the telltale signs of drug use. But as my friend Anne discovered, turning a blind eye to suspicious behavior only allows the problem to get worse.

ANNE

When Something Isn't Quite Right

I was the one who had to tell Anne what was really going on—and it didn't help, because she didn't believe me.

Anne came from a privileged background, but she'd also done well for herself as CEO of a cosmetics company. She lived with her son Terry, a high school junior, in an exclusive Connecticut suburb on Long Island Sound, where they had a boat at the local marina.

"Terry's doing so well," she told me. "He's so mature for his age. He has so many friends—and a lot of them are college kids, even kids from Yale."

"What does he have in common with them?" I asked.

"I don't know. . . . They just seem to like him. They drop by to see him all the time just to say hello. They'll go out on the boat for 15 minutes or so—they always seem glad to see him. And they're such nice young people."

"Anne, this isn't right," I told her. "College kids don't just drop by to see a high school kid for 15 minutes. You need to be looking into this. It sounds as though there are drugs involved."

She was furious with me. "Terry wouldn't do that," she said. "And these are nice kids. Yale students."

It wasn't the state troopers who came for Terry—and Anne. It was the FBI. The boat was impounded under the RICO statute, the federal racketeering law. Anne was charged with drug racketeering, and her lawyer told her he couldn't handle the case—she needed a RICO specialist.

Lawyers who specialize in defending RICO cases are essentially mob lawyers. Anne, from her genteel blue-blooded background, was getting more of an education than she wanted to as she was thrown in with real-life Tony Sopranos and Michael Corleones.

Terry ended up getting a plea bargain, under which he was sentenced to community service and sent to a drug rehab center for 6 months. He's back living at home now.

I had lunch with Anne recently—now that she's speaking to me again—and she told me, among other things, "I've bought a pet for the family. A German shepherd. He's an older dog."

"Why didn't you buy a puppy?" I asked.

"Snoopy has . . . special talents," she said, "that Terry doesn't know about."

She had bought a drug-sniffing dog.

MARIA

"OUR LITTLE BOY PUT US THROUGH HELL FOR 10 YEARS."

Like Anne, Maria remains horrified at the hold drugs had on her son. Though he seems to be getting his life back on track, Maria understands that her son's addiction is a battle he must face every day.

"My son is 34 now. He's been clean for 4 years now, and we pray every day that it continues—literally, every day. Our little boy who was a parents' delight—lovable, empathetic and loving, bright (scored in the high 1400s on his SATs)—put us through hell for 10 years. He was a crack addict—is a crack addict—and we take it one day at a time.

"We had him in the best rehab places. We even pulled every string we could and got him into one for professionals, like doctors and lawyers, thinking that the exchange with a different class of people would help. Of course, it didn't.

"When addicts are using, they don't care who they hurt, for the most part, even though they have an occasional pang of remorse. They are also known for using anything to get drugs, including trading a car for a few days to get a reasonable supply of their preferred drug.

"My husband had gotten me a Lexus for my birthday, and I loved that car. Our son borrowed it to 'go to the bank' and didn't come back, so I went looking for him. We live in a suburb of a large city, and I just started driving around in a widening circle.

"Incredibly, I spotted my car, followed it, and pinned these drug dealers into a parking space where they couldn't get out. I was so angry that I got out of my husband's car and told these young men to hand over the keys and, if there were drugs in there, to take them out. I told them, 'If you ever have your sorry butts in this car again, I will be sure to have you jailed for many years.'

"Looking back, I can't believe I did it. I found out later that one of them sported a .357 Magnum, and I would have been an easy victim. But I guess I just surprised them so much that they didn't know what to do.

"The interior of the car was stained and smeared when I got it back. Wet patches, gritty patches. There was no way to tell what was fast food and what was drug residue. I ended up having to pay $4,000 for a complete new interior. Needless to say, I couldn't even report it to the insurance company. I had to pay the whole bill myself.

"I have a beautiful granddaughter, and I think she keeps our son focused. He adores her, and so do I! But we've had many sad tales during those 10 years—going to crack houses, thinking he was dead for months.

"Our son was a teenager when he started with pot, and then he moved on to other drugs. Teens are so vulnerable, since they want to be accepted.

"To put some type of closure on this tale, I got a Mother's Day card this year with a note that said, 'Thanks for never giving up!' And, to put the icing on the cake, a check and a repayment schedule for everything of ours that he stole, lost, or destroyed during his 'lost years.'"

The Unthinkable

Okay, I promise this is my last example of how bad it can get when money problems get out of hand. As you can tell by now, there is almost no limit. The stories in this chapter don't happen to everyone—but they can happen to anyone. And they aren't as rare as you might think.

Credit card addiction can start the same horrible downward spiral as any other kind of addiction. It happened to a University of Texas freshman, Sean Moyer, who was a National Merit Scholar. He signed up for a credit card when he arrived on campus, which he could afford with a part-time job.

His parents weren't worried. Sean couldn't stop there, however. By the time he moved home in 1998 in a desperate attempt to try to save some money, his parents discovered that he had accumulated a Visa, two MasterCards, nine other store and gas cards, and $10,000 in debt.

He told his mother, Janne O'Donnell, that he didn't see any way out of the financial mess he'd gotten himself into and couldn't see much of a future for himself. A week later, he committed suicide.

According to the Web site Credit Card Nation, his credit card nightmare continued to be visited on Sean's parents:

> Sadly, Janne and her family are regularly reminded of their personal tragedy due to ongoing debt collection activities. The aggressive tactics of one particular bill collector were especially offensive. He made harassing phone calls to O'Donnell a year after Sean's death, suggesting that she should "honor his memory" by paying the debt. "If I had the money," O'Donnell told a reporter, "I would have paid them [earlier], and Sean might be with us today." As if the O'Donnells need further reminders of their ordeal, Chase and other credit card companies still mail "preapproved" credit card applications in Sean's name to their home.

Another college freshman, Mitzi Pool of the University of Central Oklahoma, hanged herself in her dorm room after losing her telemarketing job. But she was in a downward spiral even when she had the job, which earned her only about $65 a week. She had run up $2,500 in debt on three credit cards. When police examined her room, they found credit cards and credit card bills spread out on her bed.

It's awful and unthinkable that a child would commit suicide over $2,500. But a feeling of loss of control over money can lead to a sense of overwhelming hopelessness.

As we talk to our teenagers about money and how we handle it, we can help them establish the kinds of healthy habits that will keep stories like these from repeating themselves.

PART 3

Building
Healthy Habits

12

FAMILY FINANCES: PAYING BILLS

The top good habit you want to teach your teenagers and young adults is to pay better attention to their own budgets and expenses, which we'll talk about in the next chapter. The best way to get them started is to model that behavior yourself—and show them how you do it. They can't really understand how it all fits together unless you take them through your own bill paying and budgeting.

Maybe it doesn't seem necessary to you to go through all this when all you want is your teenager to stop blowing his allowance on pizza the day he gets it. But look ahead for a minute. Sooner or later, that kid is going to grow up and be out on his own. He'll become the head of a whole financial household and then part of his own new family unit, sharing responsibility for making the money and seeing where it goes. And whether this starts when he goes away to college or when he lands his first job or apartment, it's going to be a shock. What are all these bills? How did they get to be so high? What do I pay first? What does all this small print on the bill mean? How did my credit card get so loaded? What happens if I pay it late? Is there an easier way to do this?

No one should go out into the world unprepared for something he's going to have to face every month, with no letup and no vacation ever. And the frustration that comes from being unprepared is so unnecessary. Your teen has the perfect classroom for building good habits in bill paying, budgeting, and money management right in your home, at your own kitchen table, or wherever it is that you sit down to pay the bills each month.

Here is what you'll need for your classroom.

- The whole family, at least everyone age 12 and over. It's okay if you include the younger ones, too; in fact, it's a good idea. Don't worry about overwhelming them. If they're too young, they won't follow it. If they're old enough to follow it, they're old enough to start joining in as part of the family's financial team.

- All your monthly bills.

- A calculator.

- Whatever you use for the actual mechanical process of paying the bills—a computer or pens, envelopes, and stamps.

- Something to write on. It's best to use something big, like a blackboard or a flip chart and an easel, but a legal pad or a computer screen will work just fine, too.

- Some scrap paper for calculating and taking notes.

As many kids as you have at the table, assign everyone who's old enough a task—operating the calculator, writing things down on the flip chart—even stuffing envelopes. You want everyone to be involved.

This bill-paying evening should become a regular monthly routine. I'll lay out the program for the first one, because there are some things you'll have to set up.

Bring in one of your paycheck stubs. That's right—you're going to start with what you have to work with, the money you take in. Show your kids all the figures—the gross pay, the deductions, the net pay.

Have the kid who's handling the job write down these figures and the kid who's handling the calculator subtract the deductions from the gross total. I don't expect he'll find that there are any mistakes, but it's a good way to get started. You'll want to explain what all those deductions are. In the case of the payroll tax for Social Security, explain how that gets withdrawn up to a given maximum and then is removed from your deductions (or, if it's late enough in the year, explain that it was there earlier and show your teens a paycheck stub that included it).

Category	Item	Amount per Month	Total per Month
Gross Income (Regular)			
	Mom's check	$	
	Dad's check	$	
	Other	$	
			$

Multiply the paycheck by four (if a weekly paycheck) or by two (if biweekly) and put the total in the first section of your chart—"Gross Income"—along with any other regular income. Explain to your kids that these figures can change if, for example, someone gets a raise, someone changes jobs and takes a pay cut because it's a better opportunity in the long run, or someone gets laid off or gets sick and can't work.

"Other" income is whatever other income your family gets regularly—stock dividends, Social Security, child support, and so forth. If it comes at more widely spaced intervals, such as quarterly or annually, average it by month.

The deductions will go in the second section of your chart, which you'll mark "Payroll Deductions."

Category	Item	Amount per Month	Total per Month
Payroll Deductions			
	Federal income tax	$	
	State income tax	$	
	FICA	$	
	Medical insurance	$	
	Other	$	(Gross income less expenses)
			$

Fixed expenses go next on your chart. These are the ones that are inexorably built into your budget. They're the things that your family can't do without and, for the most part, can't skimp on. Your mortgage and property taxes are fixed expenses. So are your heating, electric, and water bills. Your kids' educa-

Category	Item	Amount per Month	Total per Month
Fixed Expenses			
	Mortgage	$	
	Escrow for property taxes	$	
	Auto loan	$	
	Heat	$	
	Electric	$	
	Water	$	
	Tuition	$	
	Credit cards (existing balance)	$	
	Telephone	$	
	Cable TV	$	
	Internet access	$	
	Other (itemize)	$	
			$

tion and your car loan are, too. And although you may think that in a pinch you could do without cable TV and Internet access—and, on some days, even the telephone—if you have them, they are considered fixed expenses.

You can quibble to one degree or another about any of these. Your heating and electric bills may vary from month to month, and you could conceivably lower them by installing energy-saving devices.

If your kids are in private schools, you could take them out and put them in public school or a state college or a community college. You could get a less expensive car.

For that matter, you could sell your house and move into a small apartment.

There's nothing that can't be negotiated. But, for now, these are the fixed expenses for your household. You've made those decisions about where you're going to live; you've made those decisions about the kids' education.

The kids are starting to see where the money goes. (So are you, if you've never done this before. Teaching someone else is always the best way of learning.)

Fixed expenses are the ones that are sitting there in front of you when you go pay the bills. When you're done writing out the checks (or the electronic equivalent), you're finished with the fixed expenses. It's time to total up that list, subtract from the income, and pay those bills.

Okay, that money's gone. Out of the equation.

Now, let's see what you have left.

Variable Expenses

You're not finished with your expenses, not by a long shot. Notice any important omissions? Your kids certainly will. What about eating? Speaking of which, I'm hungry. When are we going to be finished with this and grab a bite to eat?

But it may not go like that. Hopefully, you've ordered in pizza, knowing that this process is going to take awhile. For another, you may well be discovering that your kids are finding this a fascinating, if a little scary, experience.

And they're right. We've left out some very important stuff,

What about Credit Card Bills?

You have to pay them every month. That ought to make them fixed expenses, shouldn't it?

Does that mean that all you have to do is put that late-night pizza on your charge account, and it becomes a fixed expense?

Not quite.

When you start working on your budget and putting together this chart, anything that's on your credit cards is a fixed expense, and it remains that way until you have the debt paid off.

But new charges are not. They have to be budgeted as variable expenses. You have to decide what you can afford—and what you can't—*before* you put the expense on your credit card.

some necessities. Food and clothing. But these, and everything else you plan to spend this month, are variable expenses, because you have to budget them out of whatever's left over.

Now it's time to make a list. What do you spend money on every month?

Actually, this is a two-step process, so here's where the scrap paper comes in.

First, write down everything you can think of that you spend money on. Let the kids do it first. We need groceries; we need clothes; we need to go to the movies; we need to eat out one night a week. They'll come up with a pretty good list, but what do you want to bet they'll forget toilet paper, dishwashing detergent, and paper towels?

But eventually, you'll have a complete list of likely expenses for the month—on scrap paper.

Now you just have to organize the list.

Your kids may have said that they need food and they need to go to the movies. Actually, though, they need the first but don't need the second.

So on the "variable expenses" list, we now separate out variable necessities from luxuries. Have whoever's keeping the list put a check mark next to the necessities—they need to be budgeted for first. How much should be set aside for them? Well, all these expenses need to come out of what's left over after the fixed expenses are paid. And they have to be estimated based on a sense of how much things cost and how much your family needs on the average.

This is why it's a good idea to start budget talks when your kids are young—your little ones will go to the supermarket with you, but your teenagers won't.

With teens, cut to the chase. Have your typical shopping budget ready—food, housewares, clothing, and any other variable necessities that are part of your household needs. These are the figures that will go in next.

Category	Item	Amount per Month	Total per Month
Variable Necessities			
	Food	$	
	Housewares	$	
	Clothing	$	
	Other (itemize)	$	
			$

Obligations

Are we at the luxuries yet?

Not quite.

Next come the obligations. They're not fixed expenses, in the sense that they aren't represented by that pile of bills on your table. They are, however, absolute obligations. You build them into your budget, and you protect them by whatever means necessary.

I'm talking about your savings obligations and your charity obligations. Savings is one, because you owe it to yourself; charity is another, because you owe it to your community, your faith, or whatever represents your connection to the fact that we aren't islands, that we're part of something greater.

If you're giving your kids an allowance, that can go in this section, too. This includes a regular weekly allowance or clothing and schoolbook allowances.

Turn to page 188 to see what the whole chart looks like.

What's left is pocket money for luxuries—family luxuries, like a movie-and-pizza night out, or medium-term savings for family luxuries, like your family vacations. And pocket money for you, the parents. You're the ones who are earning the money that's being apportioned. The kids' extra pocket money, over and above their allowance, can come from earning it themselves.

Doing It Better

Is everyone satisfied with the way the money is budgeted? Does anyone have any ideas about how it can be done better? If you have teens in the house, the answer will be yes. Teens always know a way that it can be done better.

This is the time to discuss it. In any project such as this one, when you're sitting down with your kids and discussing money, talk about the theory as well as the practice. Don't just slog

Category	Item	Amount per Month	Total per Month
Gross Income (Regular)	Mom's check	$	
	Dad's check	$	
	Other	$	
			$
Payroll Deductions	Federal income tax	$	
	State income tax	$	
	FICA	$	
	Medical insurance	$	
	Other	$	(Gross income less expenses)
			$
Fixed Expenses	Mortgage	$	
	Escrow for property taxes	$	
	Auto loan	$	
	Heat	$	
	Electric	$	
	Water	$	
	Tuition	$	
	Credit cards (existing balance)	$	
	Telephone	$	
	Cable TV	$	
	Internet access	$	
	Other (itemize)	$	
			$
Variable Necessities	Food	$	
	Housewares	$	
	Clothing	$	
	Other (itemize)	$	
			$
Obligations	Retirement savings	$	
	College savings	$	
	Charity	$	
	Allowance	$	
			$

through details. Relate it to their own budgeting that they need to do now, that they'll be doing more of as high school seniors and still more of in college, and that they'll eventually be doing on their own. Show them how the same principles that apply to the simple budgeting of a junior high school allowance will carry forward to more complicated budgets. Make sure they understand that if they take it step by step, they'll master every step of the process.

In discussing how your budget can be retooled, remind your kids that it's parents' money, parents' choices, but that their input is welcomed and appreciated, and will be taken seriously. Remind them also that their expenses are figured into the budget, and that what's left over is the parents' discretionary income, not a bonanza for them—although if they figure out better ways to economize, there'll be more for enrichment, vacations, and their college funds.

They have ideas about how to cut back on food expenses? Sounds good. What are they? How about everyone takes turns shopping for the week and see who can come up with the healthiest, tastiest meals on the cheapest budget.

How about the fixed expenses? Can they be discussed? Is it possible to cut back on fixed expenses, or are they . . . fixed?

You bet it's possible.

There are four different kinds of fixed expenses.

Fixed in stone. These expenses are your taxes and payroll deductions. You have no control over them; you're just going to have to take them off the top every month. Most of us need to put our mortgages in that category, too—they'll get paid off eventually, but not while our kids are still in the house.

Fixed in mud. On the next level are those payments that are "fixed in mud." You can get out of them, but not right away—it'll take some heavy slogging. Car payments fit in this category. So does revolving credit card debt. You can get out of it by paying more than the minimum every month (and you *must* do this in order to get ahead). If you've accumulated a lot of debt, however, it may take awhile.

Fixed in water. These payments are for things you need, but maybe you don't need so much of it. What payments can you cut down on? The family can put your heads together on this one. Phone bills, maybe. Make it a goal to cut down on your long-distance bills by 25 percent. Maybe you could place an egg timer by the phone as well as a reminder of what are peak hours and what are cut-rate hours. Utility bills? Turn off more lights? Yes, you've thought about all this before, and no one does anything about it. But the truth is, it's a virtual psychological impossibility to remember to turn off lights if you're not paying the electric bill. Your kids still won't actually be paying the electric bill, the water bill, or the phone bill (unless you devise a system for charging everyone for his own long-distance calls). They will, however, be part of the process of paying. And that can sometimes make a real difference.

Fixed in sand. These payments are fixed this month, because the bills came in and you have to pay them. They can change next month, though. You can cut off the premium channels on your cable service. You can even cut off the cable service, for that matter. You can stop charging pizza on your credit card.

For some families, the "fixed in water" expenses are more like "fixed in quicksand," which is what my friend Darla named it. That's when expenses don't have to be so high, but they are, and no one's doing anything about it.

DARLA

"$30 A MONTH"

Darla is a 43-year-old CPA and single mom from Scottsdale, Arizona. Her electric bills were out of control because of the age-old "Can't you ever turn off a dog-gone light switch??" syndrome, carried to an extreme.

"I don't know if my daughter Hannah has ever turned off a light in her life. I used to nag her about it a lot, but it never did any good. When she was littler, she'd say, 'I'm afraid of the dark.' When she was a little older, she said, 'I just don't like to be alone—having light in the house makes me feel safer.'

"'Even when you go out?' I'd ask her.

"Then she went through the phase, of course, when her answer to that (and everything else) was 'Why don't you leave me alone! I hate you!' *Slam!* (leaving behind her, needless to say, a house lit up like Rockefeller Center at Christmas).

"I often wondered how much her switched-on profligacy was costing us. When she went away to college, I found out: It came to about $30 a month.

"As it turned out, after her first semester, Hannah moved back home to save money, and that was when I confronted her with the difference in the bills.

"'I'll try to do better,' she promised.

"I liked that a whole lot better than I *hate you—slam!*, but I still wasn't satisfied. It still felt to me like the electric bills—and other utility bills—were a morass of quicksand that the household could very easily descend back into.

"So I tried one of Neale's suggestions. Why not? I'd used a lot of them in the past, but for some reason never this one—although it had always seemed like a good idea. The penalty jar, or as I called it, the *quicksand jar.* I set it up in the kitchen, and anyone who walked out of a room and left anything on, whether it be the lights, the stereo, the TV, had to put a quarter in the jar.

"I asked Neale about this at a seminar she gave— how had she come up with the amount? She told me, 'It was after deep thought and a very scientific study, which consisted of putting a jar on the table and saying, "Okay, it's a quarter." But it turned out to be just the right amount, for two reasons. If someone walks out and leaves a light on four times during a day, it's a dollar, so by the end of the month, they've made up the extra 30 smackers on the electric bill. Or they can hit the trifecta by leaving the lights, the TV, and the stereo on all at the same time, or the quadrifecta. Is there such a thing? There is in our house.'

"The second reason why it's a good idea is that no one's going to argue over a quarter. This is especially useful, Neale pointed out, if you have two kids, as she does. 'Instead of "You did it!" "No, you did it!" "You were the last one out of the room!" "No, you were!" I put a stop to all that by simply saying, "Both of you put in a quarter."'

"In my family, after we instituted the rule, Hannah used to delight in catching me—howling with delight if I left the kitchen to go to the bathroom and didn't turn out the light. Did I pay? You bet I did. It helped reinforce the rule. And what the hey, it was only a quarter.

"Can this approach backfire? That's actually what Hannah asked me, and as a matter of fact, my husband, John, asked the same question. Isn't it true that turning a light off and on costs as much as leaving it burning for 15 minutes.

"Neale says no. But I'm from Missouri, so I researched it myself—and she's right. That's an old wives' tale (or in this case, an old husband's and daughter's tale). If you don't believe me, check the Web site for your local utility company, under money-saving tips.

"It doesn't backfire. And after a while, it really does result in fewer lights being left on."

Financial Planning in the Future

If you pay your bills the old-fashioned way (write checks out, fill out the check ledger, put checks in envelopes, take them out to the mailbox), that's fine. It's good for your kids to know how to do that. But they should also be learning about electronic banking and personal financial software like Quicken or Microsoft Money. After all, they're growing up in the 21st century.

Now you can bring out the ice cream and chocolate sauce. It's all over . . . for this month. You'll all be back around the same kitchen table, same time next month. But the more your kids do it now, while you're still there to help them, the more it will be natural for them when they're doing it on their own. And, a side benefit, the more they'll understand that you're not made of money.

AMY

A Shaky, Out-of-Control Feeling

Amy and her daughter Joanie began working on a budget by sitting down and paying bills together. Amy instant-messaged me via her computer to tell me that Joanie would be coming over that night to begin working on it. They had decided that Joanie would move back in with Amy temporarily so that they could work together at getting out of debt and putting some financial stability into Joanie's life. I told her that I'd be on-line that night in case she needed support.

I heard from them not long after they'd started the project.

AMY: *We aren't coming along too well. I haven't factored in increasing hours worked, but the numbers right now are just plain dismal, and I have that shaky, out-of-control feeling. We'll start the No-Magic-Money Log tomorrow, but right now I feel hopeless.*

I told Amy to give me the numbers, and we started by figuring out their combined income. She said that she takes home about $2,500 a month, after taxes and an automatic payroll deduction for her car insurance. Joanie currently makes $900 a month working part-time, so their combined monthly income is $3,400.

Next, we added up their monthly expenses. For the next 2 months, Joanie would be paying $200 a month rent and half of the utilities at the apartment, which was $102. Amy's mortgage is $1,034, and her electric, water/sewer/garbage, phone, and homeowner's association dues come to $399, so together, their housing costs totaled $1,735.

Their next biggest expense was for their cars. Gasoline and car upkeep, such as oil changes, averaged about $80 for each of their cars. They also were each still paying on their cars: $245 for Amy's Mazda, and $360 a month for Joanie's Tiburon. They both realized Joanie's car was too expensive (it had been one of her ex-husband's extravagances), but they were stuck with it because they couldn't get what they still owed on it if they tried to sell it or trade it in. In all, their car expenses totaled $765.

Then there was an assortment of other expenses. Personal items such as haircuts, clothes, cosmetics, and Amy's prescription medications came to $170. Amy's monthly payments to the IRS and to a local college for a class she took last spring totaled $140. So with housing, car, and miscellaneous expenses, their combined monthly total came to $2,810.

We were now ready to discuss her credit card debt. I told Amy she couldn't go on paying the minimum she owed, so we rounded her payments up to $325 on Discover and $100 on Amex Blue. I advised her to pay off her MasterCard total, which was $611. The time had come to find out the grand total.

NEALE: *It comes to $3,846—we'll round it up to $4,000. And you bring in $3,400. So you have to find a way to get an extra $600 a month. And frankly, that's not so awful. I was expecting worse. So let's take a look at it. Joanie makes $900 a month. If she gets a full-time job at, say, $1,500 a month, that makes up the missing $600 right there. In October, you lose the rent at Joanie's apartment, which puts you $200 ahead. And if you take in a boarder for your spare room, which we discussed, at $300 a month, you're already $500 in the black, before you even take a second job. Now, you said one more nursing shift for you would be how much?*

AMY: *About $1,200 gross. I don't really know what it will do to my taxes.*

NEALE: *We'll take a conservative guess and say you take home $800. That moves you from $600 in the red to $1,300 in the black, which should be a little less scary. Let's cover one more thing. Do you know the single greatest return on investment, guaranteed, that you can get? Ask Joanie, too.*

AMY: *We don't know.*

NEALE: *Okay, here it is: paying off your credit cards. There's no investment you can make that will earn you as much interest as you're paying. The $600 that Joanie charged on meals and whatnot—if you pay it off at the minimum, you guys will be paying on the principal for the rest of your life and hers. So the first thing you need to budget in, once you get the income, is paying extra on those cards each month.*

AMY: *We just talked about it . . . and we both agree with you.*

Paying the Minimum

Figuring at a typical credit card interest rate of 18 percent, and a minimum payment of 2.5 percent, here's what happens to a debt of $4,000.

It will take you nearly 25 years, and $5,615.32 in interest to pay off the debt if you pay the $100-a-month minimum. To make the point completely clear, that's not total. That's just interest. Altogether, you'll be paying the company $9,615.32 for your $4,000 worth of stuff.

And if you get carried away and put yourself $10,000 in debt?

Your minimum payment is up to $250 a month, and you'll pay it off in 32 years, along with $14,615.49 in interest.

NEALE: *Good. And she understands more or less how it works?*

AMY: *Yes—which she didn't before. Okay, I do feel a little better, but it's the emergency stuff that still panics me.*

NEALE: *Yes. And that's why, even though paying down credit card debt is a very high priority, getting $2,000 in a savings account is even higher. Now let's make a timetable. Joanie gets a full-time job . . . when?*

AMY: *She's probably not going to change jobs for at least a month. She could get a second job after mid-August.*

NEALE: *So by the end of August, she's setting a goal of making $600 a month more?*

AMY: *Yes.*

NEALE: *And you?*

AMY: *I'll contact the nurse manager at the hospital tomorrow. I should have a new shift within the next couple of weeks.*

NEALE: *The spare room?*

AMY: *That will probably take longer, since there isn't a bed in there, and I haven't painted it yet, and I've been using it for storage space.*

NEALE: *Beginning of September?*

AMY: *Sounds reasonable.*

NEALE: *So by the beginning of September, you have the plan implemented. Your debt, over and above your month-to-month expenses, is about $10,000. That means if you don't run up any more debt, you can get out of debt and have at least $2,000 in savings in a year. Nursing's a hard job, and working an extra shift for a year is going to be a killer.*

Paying a Little More

Let's take another look at a $4,000 debt.

If you pay $25 over the minimum—that's two movies with popcorn and a soft drink per month—that 25 years shrinks to 44 months, and the interest comes down to $1,490.22.

If you pay $50 over the minimum—a ticket to a Dave Matthews concert—you're down to 35 months and $1,146.71 interest.

And if you can make it $75—two new sweaters—now it's 29 months and $935.15.

AMY: *I can do it.*

NEALE: *I know you can. There's nothing you can't do. But give yourself a bit of a break. And allow yourself some time for false starts and occasional screwups, which happen to everyone, and you're still looking at being free and clear of debt, and putting money away, within 2 years easily.*

Amy found out that not every part of every plan works for everyone. For instance, even though her house was set up in such a way that renting her spare room out was feasible, that part of the plan didn't work for her. The boarder wasn't a good fit, so after about 6 months, Amy asked her to find a new place to live. The income helped, but it wasn't worth it. But overall, the plan put her and Joanie on the right path and back in control of their lives.

13

GETTING TEENS INVOLVED WITH THEIR OWN EXPENSES

What should your teenager be paying for—and what should you be paying for? To what extent should your teen be involved with managing his own budget?

The teen years are the dress rehearsal for real life. We all have a burning parental desire to shield our children, to guard them from pain and suffering, to protect them from the harsh realities of life. But by the time they're teens, some of the harsh realities of life are there, and the others are around the corner. And there's no better anchor for a teenager than learning to take financial responsibility.

You're still responsible for your kids' basic needs—shelter, food, clothing, and education. Even so, opportunities to teach your kids' how to manage money do exist.

Shelter and Food

As far as shelter is concerned, those decisions remain entirely in your hands. When your kids are involved with the bill-paying process, they'll have a sense of how much shelter costs and how it fits into the overall budget. You'll want to talk about all aspects of finance when you do those bill-paying sessions, including how a person qualifies for a mortgage and gets approved for a home loan, and what portion of a person's income should go for shelter.

Teens tend to assume that they'll make a lot more money than they actually will, especially in their early years, so a realistic discussion of income and outgo is in order. For the most part, children tend to shy away from lectures that begin with "When I was your age . . . " They may be more receptive to reminiscences, however. Your teens may be fascinated to hear about your first apartment—how you found it, how you furnished it . . . and how you paid for it.

As for food purchases, although most of the responsibility rests squarely on your shoulders, it's okay for teens to share the burden in certain situations. Unlike shelter, food can be a basic need *or* a want. We must eat each day just to survive—and the healthier the meals, the better. Yet, food can be a treat, a form of instant therapy (we all have our comfort foods), or a tool of social interaction, a way to get together with friends. You're responsible for the necessity part—three square meals a day and probably some healthy snacks. You're not responsible for candy bars or pizza with the gang.

Clothing

Like food, clothing can be a necessity or a luxury—and a shared responsibility. The challenge here is that teens not only think they'll make money more than they will, they also tend to think that things cost less than they actually do. That often means that teens make their purchasing decisions by the tag that gives the name of the designer, rather than the tag that bears the price.

And that's all right. There's nothing wrong with having good taste or developing your own personal taste. But teens need to know what things cost, and how much more certain things cost than certain other things.

You're responsible for making sure that your teen has clothes that fit; that are warm in the winter and cool in the summer; that are dressy for weddings, funerals, and job interviews; and that are casual for hiking, jogging, and crawling under a car to change the oil. You're not responsible for making sure they have a Prada label on them.

One of the best ways to handle the development of teenage responsibility in budgeting, spending, and decision making is right here.

Figure out an appropriate budget for outfitting a teenager. You know how to do that—you've been buying kids' clothes for years. You know how many outfits they need, what kind, and how much they cost.

This is a good time to get your teen his first stored-value card, low-limit credit card, or secured card—in the amount of money that you're giving him for clothes. It's okay to be a little too generous. You can build in a little fail-safe cushion if you want. Shirts do get ruined, and sometimes it's nobody's fault. But it's very important that you don't give too much, because that will kill the whole point.

Explain to him the terms of the deal. The money is being given to him as his clothing allowance for a specified time period. I'd recommend 3 months for a younger teen with very little experience in budgeting, 6 months for an older teen. Three months will take him through one season. It will involve some real decision making. If he screws it up—and a lot of people screw things up the first time—he'll learn from it, and the shorter time frame means that it won't be calamitous.

For the older teen, the lump sum will be greater, and the choices will be more complex. A 6-month time span means a couple of seasons. It means being cognizant of December even though it's only July. It means not spending the whole clothing allowance at once.

If the money is put into a stored-value account, the benefit is that it won't be cash that he can lose. Plus, he'll be able to keep track of exactly what he's used it on—and so will you.

He'll have enough money in the account to pay for serviceable generic brand products. If he wants to spend $50 for a pair of Fossil jeans as opposed to $25 for a pair of JC Penney jeans, that's his choice. But he'll have to understand that he'll be limiting the number of purchases he can make if he opts to buy designer items.

Education

Secondary school is your responsibility, and if you want to send your kids to private school, that's your choice and still your responsibility. That includes books, and it should include some commitment to worthwhile extracurricular activities (I'll discuss this in more detail below).

I believe that all parents, no matter how tight their financial pinch is, should do whatever they can to help their kids out with college. You can do only so much, however, and—very important—shouldn't shortchange your retirement fund; that comes first. But I really do believe that college remains part of a parent's core responsibility.

By the same token, I believe that kids have to take responsibility for their own college education—and it doesn't matter how comfortably fixed the parents are. Even if you can pay for 4 years at Stanford, you shouldn't.

I believe that kids should be prepared to pay one-quarter of their college expenses, whatever they are.

In the case of a state college, at current rates, that figure comes to approximately $2,000 to $2,500 a semester, including tuition and fees, for a student living at home (it varies from state to state, but this is the general range). For a community college, it's less—from $1,500 to $2,000.

At the higher end of the spectrum, MIT weighs in at about $38,000 per year. So the range is extraordinary for U.S. colleges—about $4,000 to $40,000 a year.

That means that your prospective college student would be responsible for from somewhere in the range of $1,000 to $10,000 a year.

Most teens should be able to earn enough to pay their freight free and clear on the low end. On the high end . . . no way.

But coming up with the cash for tuition is only one way for a teen to contribute to her college experience. Scholarships and grants count. So does getting a college loan. So does getting into an accelerated program and graduating in 3 years.

The contribution is what's important. Your child has to be a part of her own education, to share the responsibility, in whatever proportion you divvy it up. The sharing is key.

It's not unreasonable to ask your teen to make this contribution, and you should do it, even if you can afford to pay. There's nothing wrong with sending your teen to an elite school if she can get into it and if you can afford it. If she can get into an MIT or a Princeton, even if she doesn't get a scholarship, that's an achievement, and it should be honored. But it still shouldn't be a gift.

A quarter of the tuition to an elite college is a substantial commitment in student loans, but a degree from an elite university is a substantial asset.

There's no guarantee of success in anything one does in life, and you can't guarantee, or get a guarantee, that your child will do well in college. But there's always more incentive to succeed at something that a person has a financial stake in.

Some Ways of Saving for College

UTMA accounts. Some parents, grandparents, or other concerned adults elect to provide for a child's college expenses by creating a custodial account using the Uniform Transfers to Minors Act (UTMA—formerly known as UGMA, the Uniform Gifts to Minors Act). This is essentially a way to create a trust for a minor without actually going through the legal rigmarole of creating a trust, which tends to be more expensive, complicated, and time-consuming than a custodial account. The money belongs to the minor, but it's still managed by the custodian.

This can be a good thing because of its definite tax advantages. It can be a bad thing, however, if you're not sure how responsible your child is, because when the child attains legal majority (21 or 18, depending on the state), all the money belongs to him. It can be a problem for another reason: Having money in a custodial account can make it more difficult for the child to get financial aid when applying to college. There's no one yardstick to say whether or not a UTMA account is right for you, so it's best to go over your particular situation with your financial consultant.

529 plans. Individual states offer these plans, which are designed to help families save for future college costs and which offer tremendous tax breaks. The 529 plan differs from the UTMA plan in that the money is still controlled by you, rather than your child, even after he reaches maturity, so you can make sure that it does go for college, and it doesn't jeopardize the student's chances of getting financial aid. Each state has slightly different modifications to its 529 plan (although all states have them), so you'll need to check with your own state, but essentially it works like this.

You contribute a certain amount of money to the plan. Although the amount varies from state to state, it's generally quite high—from $125,000 to $250,000.

A 529 has a 5.6 percent visibility factor, which means that

when your child actually applies to college, only 5.6 percent of the money in the 529 will count against his eligibility for financial aid.

You can actually get around that, too. If you open the 529 account in your parents' name, you can still contribute to it and get the same tax deductions you'd get if it were in your own name. But since most colleges don't require you to list grandparents' assets on financial-aid forms, even that 5.6 percent is shielded.

Your investment grows tax-free for as long as your money stays in the plan, and withdrawals of funds to pay for qualified college expenses are free from federal income tax. There may be even more state tax advantages, but you'll need to check the specifics in your own state.

Coverdell Education Savings Accounts. Also known as Coverdell ESAs, these are investment accounts that allow for a maximum annual contribution of $2,000 per student. The earnings on a Coverdell account grow tax-free as long as distributions are used for education expenses.

When Money Is Tight

Okay, kids should contribute to their own education, even if the parents can afford it. What about the opposite situation, in which the parents can't afford it?

ELAINE

"THERE WASN'T ANY TRUST FUND."

Elaine is now 37, a paralegal in a small office in upstate New York. Her stepson, James, was 7 years old when she and her husband married, and her close relationship with James has survived the breakup of the marriage.

"One of the reasons my marriage broke up was that Arnie never told the truth, and I got to where I couldn't trust him about anything.

"We have one son, who's now 10 (he was 7 when we split up), and Arnie has an older son, James, now 22, who has suffered from Arnie's lying as much as anyone. Arnie told him, James's mother, me, and anyone else who'd listen that he had a trust fund set up that would see James all the way through college and medical school. He talked about it for years, from when James was 6 and Arnie and I first met through his senior year in high school.

"There wasn't any trust fund. I don't mean there wasn't enough. I mean nothing. A savings account with less than $200 in it. I wasn't in the room when Arnie told James. I saw James come storming out with a black cloud around his head, slam the door, and stalk off into the night. When I asked Arnie what was the matter, he said, 'He's just overreacting like a typical teenager.'

"I got the story from James the next day.

"As I said, Arnie and I are divorced now. James moved out west and hasn't talked to his father since he moved. I hear from him, though. He's working and paying his way through community college.

"Arnie's a much better father to our little boy, Sean, than he's been to James. He sees him every weekend, and he's very loving. But if he's saying anything about a trust fund, I don't want to hear it. I'm doing my best to put aside money for his college. When he gets to high school, I'll start talking to him about what will be available and the importance of working for scholarships. He's so bright. I'm sure he'll make it."

The moral of the story: You can't leave your kids with unrealistic expectations for the future. If money is tight, sit down with your kids before college—their sophomore year of high school is not too soon, or even their freshman year if they're mature kids—and discuss the options.

Do the research together. What's possible, and what's impossible? If you won't be able to afford Harvard, even with a scholarship, what about Brown, Emory, Rice, or Washington University in St. Louis? Are the scholarship possibilities any better there? What about a prestigious, small liberal-arts college like Oberlin, Bard, or Grinnell? What about a top-ranked state school like Iowa, Texas, or Rutgers?

U.S. News and World Report's annual college guide includes a list, "Great Schools at Great Prices," that always makes for eye-opening reading.

What's the best school for a teen with a special skill? Maybe that's where the best scholarship opportunities will lie.

Your home state's state-university system may be the most affordable way to go. The U.S. state-university system remains excellent, and most state colleges have campuses with particularly high reputations in one discipline or another. Find out which campus is the best fit for your teen.

Room and board is approximately half of the expense at most colleges. If it's going to be impractical for your family to pay for that, look at colleges close to home.

Don't forget about community colleges. Their 2-year associate-in-arts programs are affordable and yield practical degrees that will open doors to any number of good-paying jobs. And a young person who can't afford a 4-year college or who needs to get her grades up to qualify for student aid can start in a community college and finish at a 4-year college (she needs to make sure her credits are transferable, though).

The point is that the United States has incredible opportunities for higher education at every level and in every part of the

Look at the accomplishments of a few colleges at random that aren't named Harvard, Stanford, or MIT.

• Harvey Mudd College, California: According to Peterson's college guide, "More than 40 percent of Harvey Mudd alumni hold Ph.D.'s, the highest percentage in the country."

• Austin Peay State University, Tennessee: Graduates include Wayne H. Pace, executive vice president of AOL Time Warner; David Hackworth, author and *Newsweek* correspondent; and Valerie Moore, technologies director for the movie *Titanic*.

• Eureka College, Illinois: Graduates include former President Ronald Reagan.

• Miami-Dade Community College, Florida: Graduates include aviation pioneer Amelia Earhart.

country. With a few good professors, a library, and the Internet, your young adult can get the education she needs for success.

What about the Impossible?

Suppose after all your research, all your discussion, and your carefully considered practicality, your teen says, "I don't care. I know I can get into Cal Poly, and it means more to me than life itself, so I'm going to make it happen."

Or she says, "I'm going to graduate school for architecture in Spain, and I don't care what it costs." So you figure out what it costs. Then you point out that with the student loans she'll need and the average earnings expectancy for an architect, she'll be paying off loans when she's 50—and she still says, "I don't care. I have to follow my dream, and I'm not going to be the average architect."

What then? How much debt is too much? When do you have to step in and say, "No. I can't allow it. It's too impossible"?

Well, would you want to be the one who told Rudy Ruettiger that he couldn't play football at Notre Dame? Or Florence Nightingale that she couldn't bring nurses to Crimea? Or Denise that she couldn't attend college?

DENISE

"THEY DIDN'T BELIEVE."

Denise is one of the toughest people I know. A birth defect left her with the muscles around her spinal column atrophied. So while she was functional as a baby, it gradually became clear that she would never walk and that she would be, for all practical purposes, quadriplegic. She can operate the controls of a motorized wheelchair and a computer keyboard. I could never imagine telling her that there's anything she couldn't do.

"Growing up, I always assumed that I would go to college. But when I got to high school, it seemed everyone was discouraging me—my parents, guidance counselors, even the so-called experts who were supposed to help people with disabilities achieve their goals. Because I needed a wheelchair to get around, they didn't believe it would be possible for me to attend college. But I wouldn't listen to them.

"When I first applied to college in 1972, I was turned down. The school said it wouldn't be 'fair' to me because I didn't have anyone to help me get around campus. One of my friends wrote a letter saying that she would stay with me on campus and take me to my classes. The school then accepted me, and my friend accompanied me the first 2 days. The rest of my college career, I managed by myself or by finding the help I needed.

"In 1978, I graduated with a bachelor of arts degree in sociology. In 1995, I got my Ph.D. in criminal justice. Universities here in New Jersey, and throughout the country, have stopped discriminating against the disabled and now even offer assistance to those who need it. I know, because since 1987, I've been teaching criminal justice at Montclair State University."

What are you going to say? "You'll never be a good enough architect. . . . Don't waste your money"? "You'll never get a scholarship at Cal Poly—don't get your hopes up"? Or, like Denise's father (who came to take great pride in his daughter's accomplishments), "Honey, shouldn't you try something you can do, like stuffing envelopes"?

Make sure that your child knows the cost, and knows the risk/reward ratio. Make sure he asks the hard questions when applying to graduate school: "How long does it take, on the average, to get hired out of your program? What percentage of your graduates are driving cabs?" Make sure he insists on straight answers. If the admissions officer says, "Oh, that never happens to our graduates," there may be something wrong with that admissions officer, or there may be something wrong with the program.

Make sure that your child does the math. What is the average length of time that it takes to get a job with the degree he's going for? What is the average starting salary? Even if he doesn't stay average, he's going to begin average. How long does he have before he needs to start paying back his loans?

But if he really understands the risks (even though, as a concerned parent, you may never think he truly appreciates the risks), and if you've had the discussion of how much you will or will not be able to provide a safety net, at a certain point you have to say, "Follow your dreams, and God bless you."

Some Numbers

These are just a start. You and your teens will need to find the specific numbers that apply to their situations, but this gives a few ballpark estimates and starting points.

Perkins loans. Designed to give low-interest (5 percent) financial aid to those who are really financially strapped, Perkins loans have a grace period between the end of your education and the time you have to start paying it back. It's 9 months after you graduate, leave school, or cut back to less than half-time—longer if you're in the military.

Here are examples of typical payments for Perkins loan repayment.

Total Loan Amount	Number of Payments	Monthly Payment	Total Interest Charges	Total Repaid
$3,000	119	$31.84	$817.86	$3,817.86
$5,000	119	$53.06	$1,363.40	$6,363.40
$15,000	119	$159.16	$4,090.85	$19,090.85

Stafford loans. There are two kinds of Stafford loans: subsidized loans, which give you certain breaks on interest payment, and unsubsidized loans, which don't. Subsidized Stafford loans are given on the basis of need.

You have to start repaying a Stafford loan within 6 months of leaving college or becoming a less-than-half-time student (again, you have longer if you're in the military). If your loan is subsidized, there's no interest accrual during that grace period. But with an unsubsidized loan, even if you're not paying the principal, you're still being charged interest.

The interest rate on a Stafford loan is typically higher than on a Perkins, but it can't exceed 8.25 percent. Here are some monthly and total payment calculations under the standard repayment plan (using the maximum interest rate of 8.25 percent for student borrowers).

Total Debt When Borrower Enters Repayment	Per Month	Total Payment
$2,500	$25	$3,074
$5,000	$61	$7,359
$7,500	$92	$11,039
$10,000	$123	$14,718
$15,000	$184	$22,078

You can get more information on both Perkins and Stafford loans at http://studentaid.ed.gov/students/publications/student_guide/index.html.

What Happens If You Default on a Student Loan?

The bottom line is, nothing good. Here are the details.

- You can be sued for the entire amount of the loan.

- Your income tax refund can be withheld.

- If you're employed, your employer can be obliged to deduct as much as 10 percent from your weekly or monthly paycheck and hand it over to the company you owe the money to.

• You aren't going to get any more federal aid for any future education—or any other kind of government assistance— so don't think about going on welfare to get out from under the debt.

• You'll be stuck with any fees associated with the collection of your loan, including court costs and attorney fees.

• If you have a professional license—if you're a doctor, say—you can lose it or have it suspended.

• Your long-term credit record will be affected. Plus, you will have trouble getting future loans, such as mortgages or even educational loans for your own children.

• And after all that, you'll still owe the money.

Enrichment

School's only the beginning of it for teenagers. There's all that other stuff. Movies about teenagers being dismembered at the prom. CDs full of songs and raps that experts tell you is full of dreadful, antisocial stuff—but you don't know what to tell your kids not to listen to, because you can't understand a word of it. Demands to get holes drilled in their bodies and fragments of moon rocks inserted into them. Chess clubs and . . .

What? Chess clubs? How did that get in there?

Simple, and it's not even out of place. The same teen who's somehow figuring out a whole range of things to drive you nuts, who's flouting conventions that you had never even heard of when you were in your convention-flouting days, is doing all kinds of things that are mind-expanding, soul-enriching, and educationally sound.

Starting Salaries

To help your teen make a realistic estimate of what he can expect to earn if he graduates with his desired degree, here's a list of approximate starting salaries in different occupations for 2002 college graduates with a bachelor's degree.

Type of Employer	Yearly Salary Range
Agriculture and natural resources	$22,900–$39,000
Business	$30,000–$51,000
Communications	$24,000–$35,000
Computer sciences	$40,000–$56,800
Education	$24,600–$35,000
Engineering	$38,000–$59,000
Health sciences	$27,000–$42,500
Humanities and social sciences	$24,000–$40,000
Pharmacy (5-year program)	$62,000–$77,000
Sciences	$24,000–$53,000

Adapted from the JobWeb Web site (www.jobweb.com).

Teens' time is given over to their education, which you pay for; their amusement, which they pay for; and their enrichment, which fits somewhere in the middle. I believe that your teens' enrichment programs are part of their development into complete human beings, and they deserve our support.

There are two boundaries to this area of support, and they're both shifting boundaries. First, what's the border between entertainment and enrichment? Second, what's the border between enough support and too much?

Parents have to come up with these answers themselves. Are violin lessons enrichment, and electric guitar lessons entertainment? For me, yes. But there's no one right answer.

One bit of advice, though. Whether you're going to pay for lessons, equipment, or travel is your call. Try to make it a fair call; don't use the power of the purse to try to make your teen follow your dreams instead of his own.

Okay, let's assume that you've decided to support violin lessons, or figure skating lessons, which means a certain outlay for equipment. Buying equipment means a decent violin from your local music shop, or a decent pair of skates off the rack at Modell's. It doesn't mean a Guarneri violin, or a custom set of Graf Edmonton boots and MK Phantom blades.

At least not at first, it doesn't. But if your teen has been chosen to compete in the International Leopold Mozart Violin Competition, or has become an Olympic hopeful in figure skating, then the investment of time and money goes from modest to astronomical. And there are a lot of stops in between. The state American Legion Baseball championships, the Honor Society trip to France.

All of these are your call. But when making these decisions, you must keep in mind that these are investments that may not pay off in tangible terms. Often, measurable success in an enrichment program can mean a college scholarship. Occasionally, it can mean a high-paying career. But as it's happening, it's an expense, and this again means the ever-familiar two things. First, the money has to come from somewhere, and if a special situation means resources are siphoned away from other family needs, or other family members' needs, you must establish some sort of quid pro quo. Second, your teenage prodigy has to contribute, too.

Borrowing

Conceivably, the Guarneri and the trip to Salzburg could leave your family a little in debt, and your teen a little in debt to the family. But teens don't need to go that far to get into debt—none of us do, in fact. What if your teen, for reasons that you accept as sound, needs to borrow a reasonable amount of money? Should you lend it to him?

My belief is yes. Borrowing and repaying are the basis of credit, and every lesson that reinforces a young person's awareness of how financial transactions work is a good one.

Here's how we did it in my family, when my kids were pre-teens and young teens. A child can borrow 1 week's allowance. That's reasonable debt.

She has 3 weeks to pay it back, with interest—and the interest should be enough so that she'll feel it, and think twice about whether she really needs the loan. We made it 5 percent for a 3-week loan, 10 percent for a longer one. She doesn't have to explain what she needs the money for.

If she pays it back, she maintains a good credit rating. If she keeps her good credit rating for three transactions, she can increase her line of credit—borrow 2 weeks' allowance, with 5 weeks to pay it back. If she's late, she loses her good credit rating and has to wait through a probationary period before being able to borrow again. I think a 2-month period is a good lesson for younger kids, a 6-month period for young teens. With a good family credit rating at age 14, your teen should be ready for her first secured credit card.

For a larger loan—$300 for those new guitar amps—it's a different story. You do have to know the reason for the loan, and your teen has to present a real plan for repayment: "My band has been offered jobs playing three proms in the area, and we'll make $1,000, but we need to bring our own equipment, and our amps aren't good enough. I can repay the entire amount, with interest, by the end of May. See—I have written contracts for the three prom gigs."

If your teenager is going to borrow, it's better that she do it within the family. At the same time, with any loan that's more than just loan-against-allowance, you need to consider the prudence of the financial deal, and your kids have to understand that (a) you may say no and (b) the "no" isn't a personal rejection.

PART 4

Preparing Kids for the Outside World

14

TAKE IT TO THE BANK: CHOOSING THE BEST ONE

Your teen should be ready to open her first checking account when she's gained some familiarity with family bill paying and writing checks, and when she starts making enough money to put into it. Fourteen is probably a good age, but many teens don't open an account until they go off to college.

Whenever you and your teen decide that it's time for her to open her own checking account, the first order of business will be to choose the best bank for her needs.

Choosing a Bank

The first piece of advice to give a teen who's getting ready to open a checking account is this: Visit more than one bank.

Checkbook Basics, Part 1

One of the first things that a new checking account owner needs to know is how to write a check.

1. When writing a check, write in the name of the recipient, and then draw a line to fill out the rest of the space, so that nothing else can be written on that line.

On the next line, write out the dollar amount of the check in words and the cents in numerals, for example:

Fifty-seven and 43/100

Again, draw a line over the rest of the space so nothing else can be written in. In the space to the right of the recipient's name, enter the same amount as a numeral:

57.43

2. Enter the date you wrote the check and the purpose for which the check is being written (e.g., "Rent," "Eye doctor," "Weekly expenses"). Finally, sign the check. Your signature will be on file with the bank so it can be verified that it's really yours.

3. Now go to the check register, the part of your checkbook that's reserved for keeping track of your checks. Write down all the information you've written on the check—date, amount, payee—and also the check number, which is printed on the check.

Note: Some checkbooks are designed so that the check register is on a piece of copy paper, directly under the check. In this case, all you have to do is press hard enough—and probably use a ballpoint rather than a soft-tipped pen—when you write the check.

Make sure that you note every deposit in your check register, as well as every check you've written.

Make sure that you note every withdrawal, including electronic bill paying or ATM withdrawals.

She'll be looking at two main considerations: convenience and value. For a teenager, the easiest (but not always the best) option is to go with the bank her parents use. That's not so much different, actually, from the way most adults choose a bank.

Most people simply opt for convenience—the bank with the ATM on the corner—and it's a tempting option.

Checkbook Basics, Part 2

Besides proper check writing, another important concept that a new checking account owner should tackle is balancing the checkbook.

If your check register is filled out correctly each month, you'll be able to balance your checkbook when you get your bank statement. Here's that process.

1. Compare your bank statement with the check register. Check off, in the register, every item that appears on the statement.

2. If there are any bank transactions that don't appear in your register, add them. These can include any ATM withdrawals or electronic bill payments you forgot to note at the time, bank charges such as ATM fees or service fees, electronic deposits, and earned interest.

3. When you've checked off everything on the statement, go through your check register and see if there's anything not checked. These are called outstanding transactions, transactions that haven't been recorded by the bank yet.

4. Total up all the outstanding transactions, both deposits and withdrawals, and adjust the ending balance on your back statement to reflect them. That's your new balance.

Checkbook Basics, Part 3

Balancing the checkbook every month is a good habit to develop. But what if the numbers don't add up? If the figures don't come out right, don't panic. They're just numbers, and there are only so many things that can go wrong. Check out these possibilities.

1. Make sure everything in your statement is accounted for in your register, and vice versa.

2. Double-check your addition and subtraction.

3. Review your deposit, withdrawal, and ATM receipts to be sure you logged them properly.

4. Check for transposed numbers—yours or the bank's. Banks don't make mistakes often, but that doesn't mean it can't happen. (*Note:* If the bank transposes a number and suddenly you have a million bucks in your account, don't spend it. It's not really yours. And they'll catch the error.)

5. If it still won't come out right, sometimes another pair of eyes can help. This is a good time to call in Mom or Dad. If none of you can figure it out, ask a bank representative for help.

But it's not the whole story. And even if it were, the places that your teen needs to be close to—especially if she's going away to college—will usually be different from yours.

Before she decides to opt for Mom's and Dad's bank, your teen should interview you about why you chose it. Otherwise, she may well find herself in the situation of the little girl whose mother sliced off each end of the roast before putting it in the roasting pan, because her mother had done it. The little girl traces this family tradition back to her great-grandma and discovers that it all started because great-grandma didn't have a big enough roasting pan.

Many of us actually did choose our banks simply because they were convenient, and we may not even know what kind of banking plan we have, besides "Um . . . checking?"

So, your teen is looking for both convenience and value—the bank that is easiest to get to and that gives her the best financial deal. If there's a trade-off to be made, it's up to her to decide which way to go.

How much is she paying for convenience? And how much convenience is she paying for? If one bank is going to cost way too much, her best bet is to put up with the inconvenience. On the other hand, if the inconvenience is really going to grate on her every time she goes to the bank, she may want to pay a little more to get rid of it. In either case, in order to know what her options are, she needs to visit more than one bank.

Following are some worksheets for teens, to help them determine their banking needs.

Convenience

Where will you do most of your banking? For most people, it's near home or near where they spend a great deal of their time—school or work. Think of this as your banking headquarters. If you're on your way to college, make sure you're choosing a bank that has branches in your college town.

Make a list of other locations where you'll want to bank. Restrict it to places at which you're likely to need access to a bank branch or an ATM more than once a month. Every bank, convenience store, and fire hydrant has an ATM machine these days, and they are incredibly convenient. But you need to know that if you use an ATM card anywhere except your own bank, you'll be charged for the convenience. Since you're going to spend some se-

ATMs

Besides high access fees, other ATM dangers exist; most of them involve ways that you can be separated from your money. Here's how to protect yourself.

• The most obvious one is don't go by yourself to an isolated ATM machine, especially at night.

• Don't give your PIN to anyone, for any reason.

• Don't accept help from any stranger who offers to give it to you.

• Don't use the machine if anything looks odd about it, or if there are any unusual instructions for its use. It's not impossible for clever computer criminals to doctor a cash machine so that it takes all your information, including your PIN. Armed with your information, thieves can later clean out your account.

rious research time choosing the right bank, don't ultimately waste all that research by paying a dollar or two extra every time you withdraw $40.

As you're searching for banks that have branches and ATMs near where you need them most, some of the following tools may be useful.

• The telephone. Check out the banks within easy distance of your banking headquarters. Call each of them and ask about branches and operating hours near your other locations.

• The telephone book. Look up the branch addresses of banks you've targeted.

• The Internet. Do a Google search on banks, plus the relevant city and state. Or try www.areaguide.net, a useful reference for all kinds of services all across the country.

Your Banking Style

The right bank for you will match your personal banking style. To evaluate what kind of banking you do, fill out the following chart.

Types of Checking Accounts

Okay, now that you know what you're looking for from a bank, what does a bank have to offer you?

MY BANKING PROFILE		
Banking Needs	**Yes**	**No**
I need a place to park my paycheck and write out checks to pay bills.	❏	❏
I need a place where I can park my paycheck and pay bills electronically.	❏	❏
I'll be paying for a lot of my regular purchases by check.	❏	❏
I'll use the ATM for most withdrawals, I'll pay for purchases with a credit or debit card, and I don't plan to write many checks at all or see the inside of a bank.	❏	❏
I'm a little nervous around banks, and I'm not sure I trust electronic devices, so I'd like to know that there's someone there whom I can talk to and ask questions of if I need to, and who might even recognize me and say hello when I come in.	❏	❏
I'll be keeping enough money in my account that I'd like it to be earning some interest.	❏	❏

Following are the kinds of checking accounts that banks offer. Check off the ones that most apply to you. When you've finished, you'll have a financial profile you can take . . . well . . . to the bank.

On the next few pages are some key questions about each checking account type to ask a customer representative when you visit a bank.

CHECKING ACCOUNTS

Does It Fit My Needs?	Yes	No
Basic Checking: This one makes sense if you don't keep a high balance but you do use checks for paying your bills and daily expenses.	❑	❑
No-Frills Checking: This may appeal to you if you don't plan to write a lot of checks and don't keep much of a balance. If you're living at home and you're not responsible for rent checks, utility checks, and so forth, you may find that you're safely under the minimum for this option.	❑	❑
Student Accounts: Some banks offer these special accounts, which don't carry any fees and may include benefits such as free checks, ATM use, better rates on loans and credit cards, and discounts on certain student-oriented purchases.	❑	❑
Interest-Bearing Checking: This kind of account can give you the convenience of checking, plus a certain amount of interest—the rate is generally tied to your balance. This is good only if you're going	❑	❑

Basic Checking

- Do I need a minimum balance to avoid fees? What is it?

- Does a second account, like a savings account, count toward the minimum balance?

- Are there fees linked to other services, like teller transactions? That is, will I be charged if I walk into the bank, go

Does It Fit My Needs?	Yes	No
to keep a substantial amount of money in your account at all times. If you drop below the minimum balance, you'll be paying fees.		
Express Checking: Good if you hardly ever step inside a bank. Generally includes unlimited check writing, low minimum-balance requirements and low or no monthly fees. But if you do use a teller, there's a charge for each visit. Not all banks offer express checking.	❑	❑
Money Market Account: A combination of a checking and a brokerage account. You can get a higher interest rate than with any other kind of bank account (of course, it will fluctuate with the market). Disadvantages: You need a large piece of change to open it, and you'll have to keep the account fairly fat. It's a little harder to make withdrawals, and there'll be limitations on the number of checks you're allowed to write.	❑	❑

CHECKING ACCOUNT SERVICES

Might I Need It?	Yes	No
Overdraft Protection: This service will cover some overdrafts, so that your checks aren't returned for insufficient funds. Make sure you understand that overdraft protection is a loan—the bank is advancing you money that is not yours, and like any other loan, it will cost you money.	☐	☐
Debit Card: You use this like a credit card, but it withdraws money directly from your checking account, rather than billing you for the charges every month. It's an electronic equivalent of writing a check. Some banks call it a check card or an enhanced ATM card or an express-checking card. Before you think about getting a debit card, you need to know that there is no grace period—you slide it through that gizmo on the counter, and the money is gone from your account. And before you use it to make a large purchase, you should know that it doesn't offer the same protections as a credit card.	☐	☐

up to the window, and have a teller process my deposit or withdrawal? What are all the fees linked to specific services, and how much are they?

No-Frills Checking

- What's the minimum balance required? (Look for a bank with no minimum.)

- What's the monthly service charge?

Might I Need It?	Yes	No
Online Banking: This allows you to perform a lot of banking services online, such as checking your balance or even applying for a mortgage, but it's most useful for paying your bills online, without checks, stamps, envelopes, and trips to the mailbox or post office. If you're going to do your banking online, make sure you can count on having easy access to the Internet. Since this probably represents the future of banking, and since once you get the hang of it it's probably the easiest way to go, it's a good idea to look into it.	❏	❏
Direct Deposit: This service allows your employer to deposit your paycheck directly in your account. There's no good reason not to use this feature if your employer is equipped to do it. It means that your paycheck goes directly into your account on the day that the check is issued—even if you can't get it there yourself—and there's no chance of it being lost or stolen.	❏	❏

- How many checks can I write for free?
- What's the charge for writing more checks?
- Are there fees linked to other services? What, and how much?

Student Account

- Will the account give me special rates on loans and credit cards?

- Does it offer incentives like discounts on products and services? Which products and services—and what kind of discount?

Interest-Bearing Checking

- What's the minimum balance to open the account?
- What are the interest rates?
- What are the fees if my balance drops below the minimum?
- What other fees are possible?

Express Checking

- Are there monthly fees? What are they?
- Are there minimum-balance requirements? What are they?
- What are the charges for teller transactions?

Money Market Account

- How much do I need to open an account?
- What is the minimum balance?
- What interest rate will I get?
- What are the limitations on my ability to access my money?

Here's a list of some other services you might be interested in, and some questions about their features.

Overdraft Protection

- What kinds of accounts offer overdraft protection?
- How much of an overdraft is allowed?
- What will overdraft protection cost me per use? Is it figured on the amount of the overdraft?
- What minimum balance do I need?

Debit Card

- Is there a monthly fee? How much is it?

- What is the monthly fee for a _____ account? (Some banks charge different fees for different types of accounts.)

- Is there a special fee for using a debit card outside of the United States?

- Will I be charged every time I use the card?

Online Banking

- What kinds of services are offered online?

- How difficult is it to learn? Can someone guide me through it step by step?

- What fees are associated with this service?

Direct Deposit

- Will this entitle me to free checking? (Look for a bank that says yes—direct deposits save the bank money, so they should be passing the savings along to you.)

Plan to visit at least three of the banks that meet your convenience test, and interview them on all these other matters. Don't forget to ask at the branch you visit whether the other branches you're interested in have the services—ATMs, tellers, bank officers—that you need.

15

INVESTING:
SOME BLUE-CHIP TIPS

The stock market can go into recession, as it did to greet the 21st century, but in general, it's a good place to go for long-term investment—a fact that is not realized by most teenagers. In a survey by the Jump$tart Coalition for Personal Financial Literacy, 80 percent of teenagers said they believed that putting money in a bank savings account was a better investment than the stock market.

In fact, putting money in a savings account really isn't investment at all. Interest in a savings account typically lags behind the rate of inflation, so you're virtually guaranteed to lose money if that's your long-term strategy.

The single most important rule for successful investment is this: Start young.

This puts teenagers in the catbird seat. They *are* young. And they need to know about compounding of interest and just how much ahead of the game they can get if they start investing now.

Around now, someone steps in and says, "Kids don't care about that. They live in the present. They think they're going to be young forever. You can't get them to pay any attention to talk about setting up a retirement plan or putting their own kids through college."

Well, I have two answers to that. First, it's not true. The future may be a bit of an abstraction to most kids, but that doesn't mean it's an inconceivable abstraction. Kids are aware of the future, and they tend to be pretty responsible people if you encourage them to be.

Second, good habits are good habits. Your kids don't need to fully understand the importance of having healthy teeth in their

The Rule of 72

This is the most vivid way of demonstrating the miracle of compound interest.

Divide the number 72 by the percentage rate you earn on your investment. That's the number of years it will take your investment to double. So a savings account earning 4 percent interest will double in 18 years—an investment earning 8 percent interest will double in 9 years.

And that means it keeps doubling every 9 years. An investment of $5,000 at 8 percent when you're 20 becomes $10,000 when you're 29, $20,000 when you're 38, and $40,000 when you're 47. And that's just the initial investment. As you keep adding to it, the money you add compounds at the same rate.

Accentuating the Negative

The Bureau of Economic Analysis, a division of the U.S. Department of Commerce, issues a regular report on Americans' personal savings rate. Their analysts subtract everything we spend money on from our disposable income, and figure that what's left over is what we're saving.

In October 2002, there was not only nothing left over, there was a deficit. Americans were saving at the rate of minus 0.8 percent.

golden years to learn that they need to brush their teeth after meals. They learn it, and it becomes a habit.

And as it turns out—in contrast to far too many of their parents and grandparents—today's teenagers *are* financially responsible when it comes to saving. According to a Harris Poll conducted in 2000, young people between the ages of 13 and 24 put 25 percent of their income into savings—a total of $54 billion annually.

Young people who are this conscientious about saving can learn to become intelligent and responsible investors.

For adults, I suggest that they begin investing when they have a $2,000 safety net, which they'll keep in savings for emergencies. Teens have fewer emergencies that they'll have to handle alone, so I suggest that they start when they have reserved $500.

What's an Investment?

An investment is any item of value purchased for income or capital appreciation.

Before I expand on that, let's take a look at what an investment is not.

Just because you spend a lot of money on something, that doesn't make it an investment. A car isn't an investment. It's only going to depreciate in value, and the potential to depreciate to nothing waits for it around every corner.

A home isn't an investment. It may appreciate in value, but that's not why you buy it. It's your home. You buy it to live in, be happy in, love each other in, and raise your children in. It's wonderful if it does appreciate in value, but that can't be your primary concern in buying it.

Here's a list of things that are considered investments.

Certificates of deposit. You get these from a bank or a savings and loan. CDs are interest-bearing, FDIC-insured "debt instruments." This means, essentially, that you're loaning money to the bank, and you'll be paid back with interest after a certain period of time—anywhere from 3 months to 6 years—which is why they're also called "time deposits." They are low-risk, low-return investments.

Appropriate for teens? Yes, especially as a first investment vehicle to show your teen how the process of investment works, and as a safe, short-term investment.

Stocks. Buying shares of stock in a company literally makes you a part owner of that company; the ownership is divided up into shares, each one of which represents a percentage of the company's net worth. Generally speaking, stocks can be income stocks, which tend to pay higher dividends, and growth stocks, which pay little or no dividends because your profits are being invested back in the company, making your investment worth more over time.

Appropriate for teens? Yes, in general, as part of a well-planned overall program. Often a younger teen may want to start out by investing in a company that she can relate to—like Nike, Coca-Cola, or McDonald's.

You're teaching your teenager two lessons—one about the economy, and the other about responsible investing. If she starts out with speculative penny stocks, dotcoms, or an Enron-type corporation—even if it doesn't end up like Enron—she's likely to start thinking in terms of "making a killing in the market," of wheeling and dealing, which is frankly not a healthy attitude for anyone, and certainly not for a teenager.

A recognizable brand name identifies the investment, in a teenager's mind, with a real product. As she assembles her portfolio, she can do so with a real concrete awareness that she is part of an entire economic system—part owner of a company that is responsible for a product she can actually use herself, and see others using.

You'll need to make sure, of course, that the company actually is a good investment.

Bonds. Bonds are debt instruments, like certificates of deposit. You're loaning money to a company or to a federal, state, or local government.

Appropriate for teens? Yes. Bonds are an investment with very little risk, and many bonds are structured in such a way that taxes are deferred; in some cases, the bonds are even tax-free. Bonds usually tie your money up for a long period of time, which is, generally speaking, a good thing for teens.

Mutual funds. These are a mixture of different investments managed by a professional fund manager and operated by an investment company formed for that specific purpose.

Appropriate for teens? Yes, after she makes sure that the fund is structured for solid growth.

Real estate. I don't mean your personal home here. This has to do with property one might buy with the expectation of making money on it, like an apartment building.

Appropriate for teens? Probably too expensive, though I've known teens who've bought run-down houses, fixed them up, and sold them. If your teen has this kind of skill and entrepreneurial drive, congratulations to you and to him.

Options. These are fairly complex stock deals in which you make your best guess as to how a stock is going to perform in the future, and then take out an option to buy or sell it at that point.

Appropriate for teens? No. Far too complicated, volatile, and risky. It's too easy to get burned.

Commodities. *Commodities* is a fancy word for stuff—actual products, like the famous pork bellies that are the staple of so many comic routines, which are bought and sold on the basis of what you think they'll be worth in the future.

Appropriate for teens? No, not in a million years. This is very cutthroat and extremely risky.

Getting Good Advice

One of the more unfortunate side effects of the go-go 1990s was a sleazy commercial in which a truck driver makes so much money playing the market, speculating, and day trading that he's able to buy his own island, actually a country. Well, banks can foreclose on islands, actually countries, too. But that guy was a dishonest fiction then, just as he would be now. You don't go into the market to "make a killing," and it's very important that teens not be seduced by this mentality.

Teens who hold back from investing in the stock market do so because they believe it's a less safe vehicle for the money they've earmarked for savings. They need to learn the ways of investing that minimize risk but at the same time give a solid rate of return.

I strongly recommend that your teenager begin his first investment account with a broker or financial planner, rather than trying to go it alone. If you have a financial planner of your own, arrange for your teenager to meet her and have a talk about different kinds of investments and different investment plans.

Your teen doesn't have to use the same financial planner that you do, but financial professionals generally won't deal with minors, and for a very good reason: They can't enter into legally binding contracts. So in some way or other, the account will have to be structured so that you bear the responsibility for it. Nevertheless, if the two of you want to, you can interview a couple more planners as well. This is certainly not a bad idea in general, because it's always good to comparison shop before making any major decisions. And it's a particularly good idea in this case, because you want your teen to understand that there is more than one approach to planning for his future.

I'd give one warning signal to parents here. You want to make sure that your kids are talking to responsible financial planners, who will emphasize low-risk, long-term planning and not get-rich-quick schemes. These schemes, unfortunately, tend to have a real appeal for many teenagers. We'd all like to get rich quick, but teens may be more easily lured by the possibility.

It's a good idea, therefore, to preview the financial planners before they meet with your teen. The other kind of planner is out there, however, which is yet another reason that you should start your child off young, so he can develop a responsible investing plan while he's still under your supervision.

If you do encounter a financial planner who tells your teen that he can double his money, and your teen's eyes start to sparkle with excitement . . . just say no. It's true, we all learn from our mistakes. But here, he'll learn more from the positive reinforcement of a good experience.

16

COLLEGE: MORE THAN JUST
THE CLASSROOM

We talk about the teenage years as a dress rehearsal for real life, and the college years as halfway into the real thing.

Your kids are still your kids. They aren't earning their own living and starting their own families yet—but they aren't living at home, under your own roof, anymore. Your day-to-day connection with them is going to change.

Many of you will find that in many healthy ways that connection stays close. There's a healthy bond between many of today's teens and their parents that's unique to this generation, based on mutual respect and genuine liking for each other. "This generation of parents is more involved," according to Jennifer Bell, coordinator of the parents office at North Carolina State University in Raleigh, as quoted in *The New York Times.* "It's the baby boomers, the soccer moms, the parents for whom the kids became their lives. Thirty years ago, parents were content to drive their kids to college, drop them off, and pick them up at graduation. Now there are different expectations, because they've been involved in their kids' lives all through school."

Cell phones and e-mail have made it easier for college kids to keep in touch with their parents, but more than that, kids today simply want to. Yale student Alexander Dryer, who says he talks to his parents at least once a day, is quoted in the same *Times* article: "Kids in my generation respect their parents as thinkers. I sort of feel like my parents are my friends. I know I talk to them in a way they didn't talk to their parents."

Of course, this is isn't true of every parent/college kid relationship, and it doesn't have to be. Many types of healthy parent-child relationships exist. With this new closeness comes a new kind of responsibility. When is it appropriate to stay close, and when do you have to let your kids find their own way?

In some areas, the boundaries are pretty clear. You may enjoy reading some of the literature your kids have been assigned and batting around ideas and concepts with them, but you wouldn't write their papers for them.

You can carry the same principle on to all other areas of involvement. It's great to be involved, but don't do the work for them. It's great to be involved, but don't live their lives for them.

The classic cliché is the college student arriving home for a weekend with a month's worth of laundry and dumping it on Mom. And the other half of that classic cliché is Mom doing it, either because she's Donna Reed and she can handle it in white gloves and a cocktail dress without so much as getting a hair out of place, or because she's Edith Bunker and she really doesn't know how to talk to her educated kids, so she just does things for them.

Well . . . no. These days, kids can figure out how to do their own laundry, and their time with their moms can be better spent discussing new theories about the criminal justice system or memories of Watergate.

I began my own experience with this in 2002, when Kyle started college in Washington, D.C.

At first I called to talk to her every day without even thinking twice about it. I had always talked to her every day, and it seemed like the most natural thing in the world to keep doing it.

Then one day when I called, she said, "Mom, I'm sorry, I don't have time to talk to you right now." I started to wonder, Was I intruding too much? Was I not letting her live her own life?

I did call her again the next day. I couldn't help myself, but I determined that I'd find out if I was being too much of an overbearing mom, and I vowed to train myself to call less often, if that was what she wanted.

"Am I invading your privacy by calling every day?" I asked.

"Mom," she said, "I'd be shocked and hurt if you didn't call. Sometimes I won't have time to talk, but that's the way it is with everyone. Sometimes I'm busy; sometimes you're busy. But I still want to know that you're there."

That was that whole conversation, and it was simple.

So I still call every day. We talk about her day, if she wants to talk about it, and about her friends and my friends. We talk about what's in the news and movies we've seen and books we're reading—the same sorts of things we've always talked about.

Your job before your teen leaves home is to prepare her for the nuts and bolts of living alone—first in a dorm, probably, and then perhaps in an apartment either on her own or with roommates. Here's a financial checklist for leaving home.

Budget, budget, budget. If your teen is used to getting a 6-month clothing allowance and paying for it with a stored-value card, debit card, or secured credit card, then you probably have no worries on this score. If this is a new concept, you need to start out with it now—it can't be delayed any longer. (For more information on these cards, see chapter 17.)

Give your new college student that card, and let him know what needs to come out of it. Be realistic here, but be ambitious. If your teen really hasn't had to budget before, and you don't know if he can handle more than a week, set him up for a month. If you think he can handle a month, give him two. If you think he can handle 6 weeks, give him the whole semester.

No-Magic-Money Log. Being away at college is going to be a wildly new experience for your teen, a completely new life situation. Even if she did a No-Magic-Money Log at home, so that she knew where her money went in that situation, she needs to do another. (See page 46 for details on the No-Magic-Money Log.)

Anyone in a new and potentially overwhelming situation needs to find ways to take control. A No-Magic-Money Log is a great tool for control.

Do's and don'ts. Well, they're mostly don'ts, but these are specifics that should be spelled out to your teen.

- Don't put impulse or casual purchases on a credit card. Pizza is the classic example here, and with good reason. Eating out because it's convenient (and without really thinking about it) is one of the fastest ways to become overextended.

- Don't buy books at the college bookstore until you've double-checked and made sure you can't get them cheaper online at Amazon.com or Bookfinder.com.

- Don't leave money or valuables around your dorm room. Make sure that your laptop computer is secure. (*Note:* A good way to protect expensive items like computers and stereos is to have them engraved with your driver's license number and the state in which you live. This can help police track them if they're stolen.)

- Do remember, in budgeting for the semester, that you're going to be responsible for expenses you probably didn't have to cover at home, like soap, shampoo, and toothpaste.

Charging That Pizza?

If you charge pizza and sodas and fast-food deliveries at the rate of $20 a week, which is about average, that's $1,000 a year on pizza and soda. If you pay it off at the minimum, you'll still be paying for that pizza in 20 years, and it'll cost you $3,000.

Dorm to Apartment

Your teen needs to know all the expenses that go into moving from the semiprotection of a dorm to the real independence of an apartment. It's very easy to underestimate the initial expenses of apartment living—"It says here in this classified ad, $400 a month. No problem—I've got $400!"

Ask your teen if she knows what the initial expenses of moving into her own apartment are. See how many of the items on the checklist on page 246 she thinks of, and what she estimates as expenses for each. Then give her the checklist, and make sure that she finds out the expense involved with each item.

Responsibility for Bills

Here's one of the most important things your teen needs to know before he moves into an apartment with roommates.

For every service that comes into the apartment—phone, utilities, cable—someone has to sign a contract to pay for the service. And whatever arrangement your teen and his roommates make among themselves to share the bills, that arrangement doesn't matter one iota to the company they've contracted with. The company will come after the person who signed the contract, and no one else. If your college student is the one who put the phone bill in his name,

Item	Expense
First and last month's rent	
Security deposit	
Deposit for phone	
Deposit for electric	
Deposit for cable	
Furniture	
Cleaning supplies	
Moving costs—professional mover	
Moving costs—renting a van and feeding friends recruited to help out	
Moving costs—borrowing a van, paying for gas, and feeding friends recruited to help out	

and someone who stayed over for the weekend made a 4-hour phone call to his girlfriend in Yakutsk, Russia, and then disappeared, there's no use telling the phone company, "It's not my fault."

A solution to this one: Use a cell phone, and don't get involved with any sort of group telephone.

But make sure your student remembers: The same is true of any bill. If he puts his name on it, it's a contract, and he has to honor it.

Roommate Contracts

The business of setting up a shared apartment is a complex one. And even though you've prepared your young adult to handle finances responsibly, there's no guarantee that his roommates come

Item	Roommate #1	Roommate #2	Roommate #3
Lease in name of			
Deposit			
Phone in name of			
Deposit			
Utilities in name of			
Deposit			
Cable in name of			
Deposit			

into the situation similarly well-prepared. So it's a good idea to make sure that everyone knows what's expected.

I recommend making up roommate contracts. They aren't binding, but at least they spell out what responsibilities have been undertaken and by whom. A good basic contract is shown above.

Check off the person whose name each of these contracts is put in, and enter the amount each has contributed to the item.

Who's bringing what into the apartment? It's good to have a list there, too—or one for each roommate. Something like this:

Item	Condition	Agreed

This can include all nonperishables that go into jointly used rooms, such as the living room and kitchen. This means items like furniture, a TV, flatware, microwave, and rugs. Each roommate should write his initials in the third column next to the item, to show that everyone agrees on the initial condition.

It's also a good idea for a young person living with roommates to put his name on everything that can't be nailed down—CDs, DVDs, books, kitchen equipment. Otherwise, even with the best of intentions and the most honest roommates, things can end up in the wrong duffel bag when roommates move out.

Along with this, the roommates should make some agreement as to what happens if an item is damaged or destroyed. Presumably, the person who's responsible should get it fixed or replace it—but what if you don't know who's responsible? What if it happens at a party?

Make a list of things that may cause friction down the line and agree on them beforehand.

- Overnight guests (on the living room couch): Are they allowed? How often? How many nights?

- Overnight guests (of a more personal nature): What's the dividing line between guest and live-in significant other? What's the agreed-on policy?

- If pets are allowed in the lease, how do the roommates feel about them? What kind? How many?

- Noise and quiet times: Can everyone agree on a reasonable balance here? (If not, you may not be suited as roommates.)

- Parties: How many? Are all the roommates cohosts? Who pays? Who pays for cleanup?

- Cleanup in general: You might want to have each roommate give a self-assessment on a Slob Index, with 1 being a tidy Felix and 10 being a slovenly Oscar. Do you all want to chip in for a cleaning person?

- Will you share food, or will all the food be separate? How about staples? Kitchen supplies? How do you work out shared expenses for food?

- What about guests? They eat too—and sometimes they don't know your rules, and they raid the refrigerator and eat everyone's food. How are you going to handle this?

Finally, it's a good idea to have a chart for ongoing responsibilities—perhaps on the refrigerator, like the chore charts you may have used at home. Maybe on a shared computer bulletin board. Wherever it goes, it should look like the chart below.

Whatever chores are agreed on may be filled in here—assigned cleaning chores or paying a cleaning person, shopping for staples, taking care of a jointly owned pet. Check off who's assigned the particular task, and then that person checks it off when it's done.

Item	Roommate #1		Roommate #2		Roommate #3	
	Assigned	Done	Assigned	Done	Assigned	Done
Pay rent						
Pay electric						
Pay gas						
Pay cable						
Pay phone						
Clean living room						
Clean kitchen						

EVVY

"IT NEVER OCCURRED TO ME."

Evvy is in her midtwenties now; lives in Morristown, New Jersey; and works as a freelance copy editor and proofreader. At the time I spoke to her, she was starting to look for a new apartment—after spending a couple of years living at home with her parents and getting out of debt.

"The first apartment I shared with friends, I was everyone's pal. Because I had a job with flexible hours, I went and signed the lease, and I agreed to stay home and sign for the phone installation, cable installation, and so forth.

"It never occurred to me that by the end of a year, both of my roommates would have disappeared into the clear blue yonder. And it really never occurred to me—I know it should have—that I wasn't signing for all of us. Just me.

"By the time I finished paying the entire rent by myself, plus all of the phone bills they'd rung up, I was out $2,500.

"It didn't disillusion me completely. I still try to be a good pal to my friends. But I make sure all the contracts are signed first."

Insurance

Does your homeowners insurance policy cover your college student's dorm room? Most policies do, but there are exceptions—and there are exceptions within policies. Consult—or, better yet, have your teen consult—your insurance agent to find out which of her belongings are insured against theft and how to protect those that aren't.

17

CREDIT CARDS
FOR EVERY OCCASION

For all the reasons that credit cards are a huge red flag for teenagers, they're still an important part of your teens' financial maturation. By the time they leave for college, they should have a healthy understanding of how credit cards work and how to use them responsibly. Here are some ways of getting them started.

First Credit Cards

Start your teen off with a card that will let her learn something about the process of charging, without throwing too much temptation in her path.

Stored-value card. Also known as a prepaid credit card, this allows you to put a certain amount of money into an account, which the teen can then draw on, using the card. In other words, it's like a gift certificate—or like a prepaid phone card. When it's used up, it's used up, unless more money is put into the account.

A good way to set this up is to put your teen's expense money—the money you're allotting her for books, clothes, and so forth—into the account, along with her own saved money (not counting the long-term savings).

A stored-value card functions like a credit card, but it has certain advantages.

First, of course, your teen can't spend more than what's there.

Second, most of the stored-value cards have online tracking capability, so you can monitor your teen's spending patterns and discuss them.

Third, some of the cards have blocking mechanisms—so your teen can't charge cigarettes, for example.

Debit card. This is essentially an electronic check in the form of a card. When you use a debit card, the money you pay for a purchase is immediately deducted from your checking account.

If a debit card is on the teen's own checking account, then he can't spend more than what he has—his balance can be checked electronically at the point of purchase.

If it's on your account . . . well, this is a bad idea. Anyone who has a debit card on your account has total access to whatever you have in your checking account.

Finally, a debit card doesn't offer the same protections as a regular credit card, so it's not the best choice if your teenager is planning to make a large purchase.

Low-limit credit card. Another option is to get your teen a real credit card with a low limit—say $300, although the companies will naturally suggest you start with more. Some credit card companies market low-limit cards addressed to "the parents of" teens as young as 15. This means that you'll have to cosign for the card, and you'll be legally responsible for it, but the card will be issued in the name of the teen, and the bills will come to her as well.

This is one of the big differences between a low-limit credit card and a stored-value card. It's a real credit card, with real bills, as opposed to the stored-value card, in which your account is debited immediately. The bills won't be super-high, because of the low limit, but your teen will have to sit down and pay them out of her own checking account—read the bills, write the checks, put them in envelopes, mail them out, and balance her checkbook.

Before you decide to go ahead and get your teen a low-limit credit card, do some checking, and make sure that the limit can't be raised without your specific approval.

Secured card. This card is similar to the low-limit credit card; however, the limit of the secured card is deposited in the bank as security. So for your teen to get a $500 secured card, you—or he—would put up $500, which would stay in the bank in a money market account, earning interest. The teen can then charge up to $500, which he pays off in the same way that he would pay off any credit card. When the secured card is terminated, the cardholder gets the original $500 back, plus whatever interest it's earned in the money market account.

These days, credit card companies specifically market cards to kids, with all kinds of safeguards built in to make sure that the teenagers don't go wild. The fact that they're doing it makes me a little nervous. These are the same companies that have historically set up their booths on college campuses to entice kids into running up any kind of credit card debt that they could possibly manage—just as cigarette companies in the 1950s and 1960s sent representatives onto college campuses to hand out sample packages of cigarettes. And, in fact, if you go the Web sites of most credit card companies and read their advice-to-teens sections, the content is primarily advice on all the smart ways you can use your credit to charge things (such as charge a large purchase at the beginning of your billing cycle rather than at the end). They tend to omit what's probably the smartest advice of all: Don't charge that large purchase—save up till you can afford to buy it.

Negotiating with Credit Card Companies

Remember—credit card companies are, first of all, good institutions. They provide a service we all need, and they can be a tremendous convenience in some areas, a necessity in others.

It's interesting how different social expectations develop. We expect auto manufacturers to build safe cars, but we don't expect them to run their own safety programs or give driver's ed classes. Nevertheless, for some reason, we hold financial institutions to a higher standard. We expect credit card companies to offer information and programs on responsible card use—and they're starting to offer such programs, although there's still a lot of room for improvement.

Whatever the card companies do or don't do, the final responsibility is ours. We can use a card to rent a car for a Florida vacation (a good idea if we've budgeted for it) or have a pizza delivered to our home (a bad idea under any circumstances), but understanding the responsible use of a card is priceless.

People, however, do get in difficulties, and though our first priority should be staying out of trouble, it's still a good idea to know what to do.

Sometimes, a credit card counselor can help. There are nonprofit agencies that specialize in helping people restructure their priorities and pay down credit card debt.

Sometimes, transferring debt can work. Many credit card issuers offer very low interest to new accounts, and people who aren't too deep in debt can sometimes transfer debt from one account to another, to take advantage of the lower rates.

But if you get in really bad shape—or if your teen does—it's important not to try to avoid the situation. Letting your answering machine screen all your calls won't make the problem go away. The first thing to do is to get in touch with the credit card company, explain your situation, and ask them to work with you.

AMY

Making the Call

When Amy and I started working together, I recommended that she call the company with which she had the largest outstanding bill and ask to have her interest rate lowered. This proved to be one of the most difficult of my suggestions for her to follow, as she told me after we'd gotten several other parts of her plan rolling.

NEALE: *Did you call the credit card companies?*

AMY: *No, I haven't. I don't even know how to start. I just cannot hear those words coming from my mouth.*

NEALE: *Tell me, why not?*

AMY: *I've had a little bit of self-respect, a tiny bit, because I could always deal with my financial crises by squeezing a little here and a little there. If I have to admit to myself that I can't do it anymore, I think I'll lose even that self-respect.*

NEALE: *What is it that you would be admitting to yourself that you can't do?*

AMY: *Keep promises. I promised the company I would pay them back at the interest rate I contracted for. What kind of person am I if I suddenly say I won't do that?*

Amy is right. It is important to keep promises, and I wouldn't recommend this to anyone who didn't really need to do it.

I always think of the inner-city youth who was in the audience one day when I did the *Oprah* show. The subject was families who'd gotten in over their heads with credit card debt, and several people on the show had complained that it was the card companies' fault. They shouldn't have sent them the cards if they didn't want them to use them, and so forth.

Finally, this youth put in his two cents.

"It's really simple," he said. "It's stealing. If you buy stuff, and you know you don't have the money to pay for it, it's just the same thing as if you walked into a store and started carrying stuff out without paying for it. If we do that in the 'hood, they arrest us and lock us up, and we don't get to keep any of the stuff. But you folks in the suburbs do it with a credit card. It's still stealing, but they let you get away with it. They give you more time to pay for it, or maybe you don't pay for it all. I hear folks here talking about 'forgiving part of the principal' or 'bankruptcy.' That's all just another way of saying, 'I took this stuff, and I ain't gonna pay,' and they say, 'That's okay. You don't have to pay, and you can keep the stuff.'"

I didn't say that to Amy. That was pretty much how she felt about herself already. And in her case, it wasn't true. She wasn't an irresponsible person, but the debt had piled up with a free-spending husband, daughters who had too much access to her credit cards . . . and the assumption that she was part of a two-income family, which suddenly changed. It can happen. So what I said to her was this:

NEALE: *That speaks very well for you—and, yes, everyone should try to keep promises and honor obligations. But in many ways the credit card business is like a giant bazaar, the kind that Humphrey Bogart and Ingrid Bergman walk through in* Casablanca, *where the street merchant tells her, "For friends of Rick's, we have a special price, and for special friends of Rick's, we have an extra special price." There are many different credit card interest rates, and there are plans that can be negotiated. If this weren't a legitimate part of the business process, I wouldn't have suggested that you do it.*

AMY: *So what do I say?*

NEALE: *Tell them that you'd like to talk to them about your loan. Tell them that it's very important to you to pay it off and meet your obligations, but you need some give-and-take here. You need a break on the interest rate. Tell them that you absolutely don't want to declare bankruptcy—you want to pay them. But you're going to need some help. And if you get a no, ask to go up to the next level of management. Just remember, you don't want to tell them, "I've become a better, more fiscally responsible person, and I'll never charge anything again if you just give me a break this time." They don't want to hear that—they want you to be responsible, but they don't want you never to charge anything again.*

AMY: *I'm going to call them right now.*

Like any experience of dealing with a big company, this one was studded with obstacles, and it had been hard enough for Amy to bring herself to try it at all. I stayed with her on instant message as she called.

AMY: *Recorded message—no option to speak to a human. Let me look on the bill and see if there's another number . . . (long pause). Finally got an option for a person.*

NEALE: Good.

AMY: *I'm being transferred to a "rate specialist."*

NEALE: Good. *So you see, there is such a thing as a "rate specialist." You're not the first person to ever do this.*

AMY: *I'm near tears. . . . I can't believe I'm doing this. I know I'm going to cry on the phone, and I don't want to do that.*

NEALE: *That's okay. . . . It's no disgrace if you do. Just remember, you're a special friend of Rick's.*

Amy was gone for about 5 minutes. Then she came back.

AMY: *Well, it's down 2 percent.*

NEALE: *That's a significant difference.*

AMY: *Yes. And they said to call back in 2 months. If I make the payments, it's likely they'll lower it again.*

NEALE: *That's great. I'm proud of you.*

AMY: *It was hard . . . and I did cry. But not a lot.*

What to Do If You Really Mess Up Your Credit

First, don't think you can take any shortcuts to getting out from under it, and don't think you can *buy* any shortcuts to getting out from under it. There are companies that tell you that they can clean up your credit for a fee, but they can't do anything you can't do yourself. What's called file segregation—hiding unfavorable credit history—is illegal, and any company that claims or hints that they can do this for you is scamming you.

Here's what the Federal Trade Commission (FTC) warns about credit-repair companies.

If you decide to respond to a credit-repair offer, beware of companies that:

• Want you to pay for credit-repair services before any services are provided

• Do not tell you your legal rights and what you can do yourself for free

• Recommend that you not contact a credit bureau directly

• Suggest that you try to invent a "new" credit report by applying for an employer identification number to use instead of your Social Security number

• Advise you to dispute all information in your credit report or take any action that seems illegal, such as creating a new credit identity. If you follow illegal advice and commit fraud, you may be subject to prosecution

Sometimes a bad credit report can be the result of an error. The FTC does offer you protection when this happens. Even though no one can legally remove accurate and timely negative information from a credit report, the law does allow you to request a reinvestigation of information in your file that you dispute as inaccurate or incomplete. There is no charge for this. Everything a credit-repair clinic can do for you legally, you can do for yourself at little or no cost. According to the Fair Credit Reporting Act:

• You are entitled to a free copy of your credit report if you've been denied credit, insurance, or employment within the last 60 days. If your application for credit, insurance, or employment is denied because of information supplied by a credit bureau, the company you applied to must provide you with that credit bureau's name, address, and telephone number.

• You can dispute mistakes or outdated items for free. Ask the credit reporting agency for a dispute form or submit your dispute in writing, along with any supporting documentation. Do not send them original documents.

The FTC recommends that you clearly identify each item in your report that you dispute, explain why you dispute the information, and request a reinvestigation. If the new investigation reveals an error, you may ask that a corrected version of the report be sent to anyone who received your report within the past 6 months. Job applicants can have corrected reports sent to anyone who received a report for employment purposes during the past 2 years.

When the reinvestigation is complete, the credit bureau must give you the written results and a free copy of your report if the dispute results in a change. If an item is changed or removed, the credit bureau cannot put the disputed information back in your file unless the information provider verifies its accuracy and completeness, and the credit bureau gives you a written notice that includes the name, address, and phone number of the provider.

You also should tell the creditor or other information provider in writing that you dispute an item. Many providers specify an address for disputes. If the provider then reports the item to any credit bureau, it must include a notice of your dispute. In addition, if you are correct—that is, if the information is inaccurate—the information provider may not use it again.

If the reinvestigation does not resolve your dispute, have the credit bureau include your version of the dispute in your file and in future reports. Remember, there is no charge for a reinvestigation.

18

GETTING A REAL JOB

If your college students' high school work experiences were "teen jobs" like doing yard work, babysitting, or burger flipping, they need to develop some skills and some basic knowledge to prepare themselves for the job market they'll be entering.

See how they do on this quiz.

The Job Search Quiz

1. What kind of résumé do I need?

a. I don't need a résumé yet. I'll worry about that after I get some job experience.

b. I should include my name and address, phone number, e-mail address, and educational credits.

c. I should include, in addition to the above, any experience that shows the kind of person I am and the kind of job I can do.

d. I need to make up some job experience, because no one's going to give a job to someone who doesn't have any.

2. The best way to get a job is:

a. Read the help-wanted ads in the newspapers.

b. Check the job Web sites on the Internet.

c. Ask my parents' friends.

d. Give some serious thought to the kind of career I want to have, target the companies I most want to work for, and approach them.

3. I'm going for my first job interview. I'll:

a. Dress casually—I want them to get to know the real me.

b. Wear business-appropriate clothes.

c. Brooks Brothers, here I come—if you don't dress expensively, they'll think you're a loser.

d. Study pictures of the top executives in the company I'm interviewing for, and dress exactly the way they do.

4. During the interview, it's particularly important to:

a. Tell a few jokes to show that I'm at ease.

b. Ask about salary very early on, so they'll see that I'm not the sort they can take advantage of.

c. Ask questions about the company.

d. Not talk very much—the more you say, the more mistakes you're likely to make.

5. Should I take an internship while I'm in college?

a. No, college is my last chance to have a good time.

b. No, I should be concentrating on my course work.

c. Yes, that way I can just breeze right into a job after college.

d. Yes, it'll count a lot on my résumé, and the real-world work situations will give me a new perspective on my classroom work.

Answers

1. Nothing should be made up. No one wants to hire someone who's dishonest. Even if it helps your child now—and it won't—it's bound to hurt him later. And he shouldn't even think about going out into the job market without a résumé.

The answer is *c,* because the purpose of a résumé is to tell a prospective employer what she needs to know about who a job applicant is and what his strengths are—not just where he lives and where he went to school. There's no one right way to compose a résumé, because we're all unique individuals. Any good résumé, however, should include the following:

- Relevant experience, whether in a paying job or not.

- A brief description of each of these former jobs and other experiences, with emphasis on responsibilities taken on and their relevance to the position being sought after. This may mean writing more than one résumé and tailoring these descriptions to the particular job being applied for. If your young adult is doing that . . . great! It means he's giving some real thought to each application.

  If he assumes that everyone knows what the manager of a Dunkin' Donuts or a camp counselor does, so he doesn't need to add a description, he should think again. The human resources manager who reads the application (if it gets that far—see "keywords," below) will want to see how those responsibilities are described.

- Relevant course work. College courses aren't the same as the real world, but they're offered for a reason, and your kid will be coming out of them with knowledge and reasoning skills that employers want. There's a reason that college graduates are hired ahead of nongrads and make more than they do.

- Anything that emphasizes strengths. Purdue University's Online Writing Lab offers a "skills list" of attributes employers are looking for. You can find it at Purdue's excellent Web site on résumé writing and other kinds of professional writing; go to http://owl.english.purdue.edu/workshops/hypertext/ResumeW/content.html.

  The site recommends that job seekers find a match between their own skills and those they believe are most desired by potential employers. They advise you to use "action words" to describe these skills.

  The "action words" on the Purdue list are verbs that proclaim positive qualities, like "accomplish" and "achieve"; leadership qualities, like "build" and "delegate"; self-motivational qualities, like "investigate" and "initiate"; teamwork qualities, like "collaborate"; and many others. The point is for the job seeker to associate himself in his résumé with the qualities a prospective employer will look for and to express them in strong, active verbs.

- Special skills. These days, computer skills and proficiency in computer programs come very high on that list.

- "Keywords." Many corporations use scanners for their first line of résumé reading. They sort out applications into ones that use keywords they're looking for and ones that don't. The ones that don't never get to the next stage. Keywords are different for each field, so your child will need to research the specific field he's applying for.

  These will include the "action words" from above, but they should also include job-specific or career-specific words for a related job. A good way to find these is through want ads. If an ad states, "Must know Microsoft Excel," it's possible that the keyword scanner for the job you're interested in will throw out every résumé that doesn't include the words "Microsoft Excel." An engineer may have to be familiar with AutoCAD. There are always new skills (especially new computer skills) that entrants to the career market need, and it's important to keep up.

The job seeker should include keywords that show he knows the field—for example, "HMO" for a hospital administrator and "competitive market analysis" for a marketing director. These aren't the tips that will get him the job, they're the tips that will get his foot in the door—or will keep his résumé from never even being read.

2. There's nothing wrong with answers *a, b,* and *c*—and your child can use all of them if they'll help. She should go to job fairs on campus, use any technique she can. But she needs to remember that it's her job, career, and future—and it's up to her to figure out where she wants to go and then take the most concrete steps possible to get there. All of that adds up to *d* as the correct answer.

How do you do all of that?

Research.

Your child needs to get a list of all the companies in the field she's interested in. There will be more than she thinks. She needs to start looking at trade and professional magazines in her field. They will give her ideas about companies, and career paths, that she has never imagined.

Then she should research those companies to find out about their products, competitors, and recent announcements, using the Web and the library. She should prepare a real campaign for the jobs and the companies she most wants to work for. Plus, all this research will help during the interview process. Companies expect an applicant to know something about their business. And the more they know, the more the employer will believe that the applicant really wants to work there—and will work hard at the job.

3. There is no "real you." Your child needs to understand that he's like everyone else—lots of different people. The "real you" that wears pajamas to bed isn't going to be the same "real you" at prom night and insist on wearing pajamas to the prom, too. LeBron James doesn't dress for work in the same outfit he wears to go out for dinner. Police and firefighters don't decide what they're going to wear to work. And your young adult doesn't need to imitate anyone else either, or wear absurdly expensive clothes. The answer is *b*. He should dress in a way that shows he takes himself, the interviewer, the job, and the company seriously.

I've done a lot of work teaching classes in financial literacy and entrepreneurship to inner-city kids, and I'll never forget the first group I worked with. They were smart, they were ambitious, they understood all the concepts I was teaching them, and they were eager to put them into practice.

But we ran into a stumbling block where I had least expected it. They drew a line in the sand about "dressing for success."

"This is the real me," I kept hearing. "I'm not gonna sell out the real me. I'm keepin' it real."

I bit my tongue and refrained from asking, "The real you is Tommy Hilfiger?"

"It's easy for you," they said. "You're an older white lady." (I bit my tongue here, too.) "You dress that way anyway."

"You think I dress like this all the time?" I asked. "You think I hang out around the house on weekends in an Alcott and Andrews suit and makeup, and my hair up in a bun? No way. But when I come here to work with you, I'm not going to wear jeans and a ponytail. It would be a disrespect for you, but even more important, it would be a disrespect for the work we're doing."

I knew how they felt, though. I remember my first job in banking, fresh from graduating college in the 1960s, still a flower child at heart. Every day I raced home to change out of my banker clothes, praying that no one I knew would see me and laugh at me.

This kind of thinking is hardly limited to inner-city black youth—and I was able to get through to them and convince them to change. More recently, I had a worse problem. I had worked with a young woman—smart as a whip, a graduate of a good college, from a middle-class white family—who was working in a bookstore and ready to make a change. She asked me if I'd recommend her for an investment-banking trainee program, and she was hurt and angered when I told her I couldn't.

"Why not?" she demanded.

Unfortunately, the answer was as plain as the nose on her face—or, rather, as plain as the tattoo of a dragon that curled down her face from the corner of her eye, across her cheek, and down to her chin.

"I can't recommend you," I said. "It wouldn't do any good. No one would take you seriously, and no one would take my recommendations seriously anymore. I can't open any door for you into a conservative field like investment banking, and I'd be hurting the chances of other young people later on for whom I could give a recommendation."

I felt sorry for her. But I didn't feel that investment bankers were a bunch of stuffy old fossils and that the system needed to be changed. It's a fine, dignified profession, and they have a right to their standards.

As comedian Chris Rock, someone who's certainly no sellout, described "keepin' it real": "Yeah . . . real stupid."

Marcus

"What do you think?"

My colleague Tad taught college-level courses in the New York State prison system for several years. Here's a story that he related to me about one of his students.

"In my first year teaching in the state prison system, I taught public speaking, and I had a student I'll call Marcus. He was probably around 30 years old, and I don't know what he was serving time for—I never asked. But he was a brilliant student. I was to have many wonderful students in my years teaching in prison, but Marcus remains special, because he had a real scholar's mind . . . and because of a lesson he taught me.

"Late in the semester, he gave a speech he had written and prepared, and after he'd finished, I told him, 'I have no criticisms of your writing or your delivery—they're wonderful. But I think it's time you started paying attention to subject-verb agreement. Listen to the "he say" and "he do" constructions, and start moving away from them.'

"This was a controversial comment, and it started a discussion that made good, intelligent points on both sides, and I let it go on for a while, only interjecting once. When one student said, 'I want to hear the real Marcus, not Marcus the intellectual,' I replied, 'Marcus the intellectual *is* the real Marcus, or as real as any other part of him.'

"But finally I turned to Marcus and asked him, 'What do you think?'

"'This is what I came to college for,' he said. 'These last 3 years have been such a revelation to me. I believe our people did ourselves a tremendous disservice in the 1960s and 1970s by insisting that using Black English was some sort of political statement. The one thing I can tell you is, when I come into this classroom, I'm not a convict, and I'm not a street hustler—I'm a college student, and that's how I want to be treated, and that's the standard I want to be held to.'

"I found out later that Marcus had come into the college program with a chip on his shoulder a yard long, angrily declaring that this was just more of the white man's shuck and jive, and he wasn't falling for it. But he did come into the program, and it changed his life . . . and maybe the lives of many others. After his release, he got his degree. He went to work as a custodian at a school for troubled children but soon became a counselor."

Unfortunately, many states today no longer have a prison higher-education program. Okay, back to the quiz.

4. The answer here is *c*. The purpose of a job interview is for the interviewer to find out whether or not the prospective employee will be an asset to the company. If she wants to find out if the interviewee has a sense of humor, she will set the tone.

Your child needs to be involved in the interview process. If the interviewer didn't want interaction, she could have just looked at the résumé or even let a scanner look at the résumé.

And the time for discussing salary requirements is after they indicate that they're interested in offering the job. But it's good to be prepared—knowing what the starting salary range is in the field and having a figure ready if the interviewer asks about salary requirements.

Here are some good tips for interviewing.

- Turn weaknesses into strengths. An interviewer may ask a question like "What do you consider your principal weaknesses?" He doesn't really want to hear, "Well, I'm late for work a lot, and I have a tendency to spill soup on my tie just before important meetings." A better way to start the answer to that question is "I'm working on . . . " For example: "I'm working very hard on my HTML-writing skills right now so that I'll understand the technical underpinning of white papers I may have to write for the company Web page" or "I'm working on my foreign language skills. I can negotiate a contract in French or Spanish, but I want to make sure my German is up to snuff, too."

• Do your homework on the company. If an interviewer asks, "Why do you want to work here?" a generic answer is a bad answer. Assume you're going to be asked this question in every interview, so have an answer prepared based on the company's goals, mission statement, and direction.

• Do some research on yourself. If an interviewer asks you about your goals, have an answer—and it should include your short- and medium-term goals. "I want to be CEO someday" is not useful information to an interviewer.

5. The answer is *d*, not *c*. An internship is incredibly valuable as a learning experience, as a way of getting to know people in that field, and as a way of gaining some understanding of how a real business environment works. It's not an entitlement or a creator of entitlements. A good rule of thumb for everyone: Never assume you'll breeze through anything.

When to Hit the Job Market

When the economy is tight, a lot of teenagers feel that they owe it to their parents to go out and get jobs as soon as they can. When the economy is good, a lot of teenagers—especially boys—take a look at good starting salaries at lower-skilled jobs or those requiring manual labor and decide that they don't need college. They can go out and get a good-paying job right out of high school, save a lot of time and money, and come out ahead of the game.

It's true that higher education gets more and more expensive, and it can take years to pay off student loans.

But it's still worth it.

Earlier, I gave the figures on how different levels of education affect a person's earning capacity, year by year. Here's another way of looking at it.

A college graduate will earn, over the course of his working life, an average of close to $1 million more than someone who graduates only from high school.

A master's degree means an average of $500,000 more than a bachelor's degree, and earnings increase by about $1 million for each additional degree thereafter.

19

THE TEEN CONSUMER: BEST WAYS TO BUY THINGS

Take a stroll through any mall in America, and you'll immediately conclude that if there's one thing kids don't need any help with, it's buying things. And if you could make yourself a fly on the wall of a UPS delivery truck and see all the deliveries of online shopping sprees, you'd be even more convinced.

But there's a difference between being a consumer and being an informed consumer, and kids have to learn that from someone. If they don't learn it from you, they'll learn it from friends. What you hope is that they don't learn it from the worst source—ads and commercials that are trying to sell them either stuff they don't need or more expensive and not necessarily better versions of stuff they do need. We all know how young this process starts. We know we can get better, cheaper, and more durable versions of products, but our 3-, 4-, and 5-year-olds won't even look at them if they don't have Barney or Barbie or Mary-Kate and Ashley on the box. Teenagers are a little more cynical than that, or at least they think they are. But they fall for advertising campaigns, too.

With younger ones, I teach the Want versus Need game as a driving game. As you pass by billboards, everyone in the car rates the item being advertised as a want or a need. If there's a disagreement, you all have to make a case for your position. This can still work for young teens—more or less up to the age when they start putting on their headphones, cranking up the alternative rock, and retreating into their own worlds. But if you have younger kids, and you start playing the Want versus Need game, chances are your teens will join in, if only to prove their superiority. And once they do, they may learn something.

A teenager with an unlimited credit card is no candidate for an education in smart consumerism, but a teenager on a budget is pretty much the perfect candidate.

Here are a few things your kids should consider when planning any serious shopping.

Brand Name or Generic?

We make most of our buying decisions before we ever walk into a store—decisions we're programmed to make. Even if we just write down "toothpaste" or "peanut butter" on our shopping list, we've already mentally narrowed down our brand choices to just a couple out of the 20 or 30 that may actually be there. Our choices are dictated by what we've seen on TV, what our parents bought, or maybe what a friend recommended, but we're almost always thinking inside some kind of a box.

It's important to make sure you know—and to make sure your teens know—that generic, or "store brand," can always be one of those choices. That doesn't mean that you have to buy the generic brand. You just have to know that it's an option.

If you're not sure, you can try it out. Buy one box of tissues or one can of soup, for example, and compare it. If it's as good as the brand-name version, go with it.

Kids like to get to the bottom of things. They're inveterate truth seekers. So have them do some product testing. You've seen ads on TV in which someone shampoos one half of her head with Brand X and the other half with Summer Exclusive Money-Swallowing Mist. And sure enough, she always ends up raving about the expensive product the sponsor is pushing. Why not try the test at home? Have a blind shampoo contest—half your head with the expensive stuff that your teens, or you, have always assumed to be better and half with a budget brand. Can you feel the difference? Maybe you can—in which case the high-priced stuff is the right choice. But maybe you can't.

Another area where the brand-name-versus-generic issue comes into play is medications. Your kids may not be ready to make that decision yet, but once they're on their own, it's one they should be aware of and discuss with their physicians.

New or Used?

Here are a couple of general thoughts on the subject that you and your teen should consider.

Is the used item going to hold up well enough? If the item in question is something you're going to use only a few times yourself, then it doesn't make a difference if you buy it used, because you're never going to wear it out. But if you're going to use it repeatedly, then you do have to ask yourself how durable it's going to be.

If you can't hit a golf ball straight, and you're going to lose half of them in the rough, get a big box of used ones. If you're a pretty good golfer, then you know that only new ones have that extra pop you need to reach the green.

If you don't cook a lot, you can consider getting a few pots and pans at a thrift shop. If you're serious about cooking, you need a new set of good utensils.

On the other hand, a good oak dining table can last 100 years even if you eat at it every night. If a used table is in good shape, it'll last as long as you need it to.

Who is it for? If you're buying a book as a Christmas gift for a friend or loved one, you want it to be new; whereas if you're buying it for yourself, a good used copy is perfectly fine.

But even in the case of gifts, that's not necessarily always true. That Hummel figurine that you spotted in a thrift shop—and that you know is the one Grandma needs to fill out her collection—will mean much more to her than anything new.

Things That Are Okay to Buy Used

High-end clothes from a good thrift shop. This isn't the era when Loretta Young could sue CBS for showing reruns of her old series, because she was being seen on TV in gowns that were no longer fashionable. These days nothing goes out of fashion; it just becomes retro. And clothes that are well-made and well-cared-for will last as long as you need them to.

Refurbished computers. If you're not among the 1 percent of the population that absolutely needs all the bells and whistles of a brand-new computer, then a refurbished one from a trusted source is often a good way to go. Computers grow obsolete (at least in some people's minds) every 6 months or so, which means that nearly new computers become available, sometimes very cheaply indeed.

How new a computer you need depends on what you do with it. I have a friend who teaches photography in college and also runs a small surveying business. For his photography work, he uses a powerful new computer with the latest version of Adobe Photo-Shop. For his surveying business, a 20-year-old Commodore 64 with 20-year-old software is all that he needs, so he's never upgraded it.

Books. They read just as well whether you buy them new or used, as long as the cover is still attached and all the pages are there. Riffle through a used book to make sure that the previous owner hasn't filled it with marginal notes—unless, of course, you're fascinated by the glimpses into the human psyche that you can find in marginalia.

College bookstores often sell used textbooks. And since the new ones can cost $70 to $80 apiece, the wise student will get to the bookstore early and snap up the used ones. An even wiser student may consider finding someone who's already taking the course he'll have to take next year and arrange to buy his textbooks at the end of the semester, thus saving the middleman markup.

Don't forget that students can also get the temporary use of books for free—from the library. And if it's a special book that the college library doesn't have, maybe the professor will be willing to put a copy on reserve to read in the library. Or if the local college library doesn't have the book, maybe another one does. Your teen can even ask his library to get the book from another one on interlibrary loan. But be aware that this process might take a few days, so he should plan ahead.

Things You Should Think Twice about Before Buying Used

Most electronic equipment. Boom boxes, tape decks, stereo receivers—these things were once built to repair; now they aren't. If they break down, a good deal of the time it's easier and cheaper just to buy a new one. These days they don't have an unlimited life expectancy.

The exception here is any item that attracts enthusiasts who upgrade all the time. If your teen has started a band and wants to buy sound equipment or recording equipment, recommend that he go for used stuff, for two reasons. First, he may not stick with it.

Most teens don't. Second, if he does stick with it and gets serious about it, he'll want better equipment—and so will every other musician who sticks with it. This means there are a lot of musicians out there upgrading and getting rid of perfectly good starter or midlevel equipment. This is true for musical instruments as well.

Note: If the price is right, and you feel like taking a chance on it, you may get lucky. For example, even though TV sets may be costly and difficult to fix, they can be very reliable, especially if they're not heavily used. I've had reports from friends whose used TVs have lasted them 10 years.

Large appliances. Generally, you probably have a better shot at getting sound used values with large appliances like refrigerators or washing machines, because they can be repaired and because people tend to sell them when they move. They're worth a lot, but not so much as to be worth moving across country, so you can often get a good deal on them.

Furniture. A young person who's furnishing a first apartment should always give strong consideration to used furniture as an option. She may be moving soon—and more than once—as she starts out in the world. Plus, her tastes may change.

But there's used furniture and then there's *used* furniture. Don't buy a used couch if the springs are at all suspect or if it looks or smells like it's been outside on the porch, getting wet and mildewy. Watch out for wooden chairs that have any give in them. If someone has leaned back in a wooden chair often, it may not be far from falling apart, and you'll never get it fixed properly.

Things You Should Not Buy Used

Mattresses. You don't know where they've been or what they've been used for. In fact, I'd recommend that if your young adult starts out housekeeping in a furnished apartment, get rid of the mattress that's there and buy a new one.

Shoes. Even really expensive ones are never going to fit right unless you break them in yourself—and they're just too intimate. It's almost like buying used underwear.

Then there are things you'd really like to buy used, because you don't really want them and you're only going to use them once, like a bridesmaid's dress, but you can't. (Fortunately, you can find ways of reusing old bridesmaids' dresses. I know some people who've cut them up and used the fabric to make pillows. If you have any friends who have done this, you'll recognize it by the pastel pillows adorned with big, ugly bows resting on the corner of the living room couch.)

This, of course, is no problem for a guy. He can just rent a tux.

Which brings us to the next issue . . .

Buy or Rent?

Rent anything that's expensive and that you'll never use often enough to justify the expense. Formal stuff, like a tux or place settings for 100 people, is on one end of that scale. Mucky stuff, like a sump pump for draining a flooded basement or scaffolding for painting your cathedral ceilings, is on the other end.

Warn your kids to stay away from the rent-to-buy or rent-to-own places, where the fine print of the contract almost always leaves you paying much, much more than the item is worth. If your college-apartment dweller wants a TV for the semester, she's better off buying one—and, as I said before, an inexpensive used one will probably do just fine.

Top-of-the-Line or Budget?

This is often purely a question of taste and budgetary priorities. You've already told your teens that you'll pay for clothes and shoes, but they have to pay extra if they want items that say Calvin

Klein or Adidas on them. And your teens have come to understand the difference and decide for themselves if they want to pay the extra. Or they're buying all their own clothes now on a clothing allowance.

The specifics of clothing decisions change over time. Paying extra for a brand name is one thing. Paying the whole tab for clothing is another.

Not only that, but the choices of apparel change. The teen who becomes a young adult and suddenly discovers that she'll be spending 40-plus hours of every week in an office will also be discovering that nothing with Fubu written on the sleeves is going to be quite right for the office environment.

Teenagers' brand-name clothing decisions are based on one question: How cool is it going to make me look?

Buying decisions in the adult world are based on another question: How good do I need it to be?

A business outfit doesn't have to be the latest thing in fashion. In fact, it's better if it's not. It should have that timeless look, the look that doesn't go out of fashion. Your young adult won't need a lot of different outfits for work, just a few that are made well enough that they'll last a long time. This, in our gender-differentiated world, is truer for young men, but even a young woman can get by with fewer outfits if they're the right ones.

A word to the wise: "It's better to look good every day than to look different every day." And it can be cheaper, too. A couple of $250 suits make a smaller dent in the budget than five $150 suits.

In addition to choosing clothing for work, a young person will also be faced with a multitude of buying decisions when she starts to furnish her own home. She'll likely have to make choices between brands that differ widely in price. A top-of-the-line vacuum cleaner, for example, may cost $2,500, but a budget brand is $200. Now, anyone is going to think that something costing 12 times as much is bound to be a lot better. In the case of vacuum cleaners, however, that isn't necessarily true. The cheaper ones may be just as good for suction and just as good for durability.

How do you know? Research. Get your facts from more than just the salesperson who has a vested interest in getting you to buy the high-priced model. Go to *Consumer Reports* magazine, or any of the other nonprofit consumer guides. See what they have to say about all the brands you're considering—and even some of the brands you haven't considered.

When do brand names really matter? When they carry with them a well-deserved reputation for reliability, a particularly good warranty, or a reputation for service. Brand names can be very important for items like personal computers. You may well need service or upgrades, so you want to make sure you've chosen a brand that will still be in existence when you need them. Fortunately, computer companies are graded every year by consumers for the most reliable service, and you can find these rankings in various computer magazines or their Web sites—PCWorld.com has a good one. Various consumer guides rate all kinds of products for all these qualities.

Another word about buying computers and planning for repairs or upgrades. They're very easy for desktops, very difficult and costly, if not impossible, for laptops.

Online or Brick and Mortar?

Online shopping is the newest trend, and teenagers are taking advantage of it at a greater rate than their elders. Credit card companies assure us that online shopping is safe—even safer than using a credit card in a store. Plus, online shopping offers variety and convenience.

Often it offers great bargains. You can comparison shop at sites like MySimon.com and Half.com. You can locate impossible-to-find items like rare books at sites like BookFinder.com. You can find discounts at sites like Amazon.com. You can bid on potential bargains at auction sites like eBay.

And you can get it all sent to your front door, without driving to the mall in a rainstorm, parking in a puddle, and getting packages elbowed out of your arms.

Just remember a couple of things.

On price: What really counts is the money that actually comes out of your wallet or goes onto your credit card statement, not the wonderful discount price that's up there on your computer screen. Is it still cheaper once you pay for shipping and handling?

Are you absolutely certain it's what you want? Because if it's not, or if it's defective and you have to send it back, will you have to pay shipping charges again?

On service: Do you need help in making up your mind? I've talked about the one-product salesperson whose main agenda is getting you to buy that one certain product. Most in-store personnel, however, are knowledgeable and helpful people who'll tell you the difference between the $200 and $350 models, and how certain features work.

Consider stereo speakers. You need to go to a store to test them to see how they sound. To buy a chair, you need to go to a furniture store to make sure that fabric colors are exactly what you want them to be, or to find out what it feels like when you sit in it.

Can you go to a store, pick the salesperson's brain, take advantage of her expertise, and then go home and find the product cheaper online? I suppose so. But don't. It's tacky. It's unethical.

On convenience: If you absolutely must have it today, the Internet—or any sort of catalog ordering—may create an intolerable delay. The best answer to this is never to put yourself in the position where you absolutely must have anything *today*. A significant purchase should always be preceded by planning and research and some time to reflect on whether you really need it.

But sometimes you have no choice. Your computer crashes,

and you have a major report that has to be finished by Thursday. Your refrigerator dies, and it's the middle of July. Then you do what you have to do.

When Should You Buy?

For circumstances other than the refrigerator in July, plan ahead. Wait for sales—that appliance can wait till Presidents' Day, Labor Day, or one of the other big sale days for appliances.

Or take advantage of sales for holidays and birthdays to come. You know who's on your list and what they want. If you see the perfect gift on sale in July, buy it and save it for December.

Plan ahead for parties or special events. Party items like chips and soft drinks go on and off sale. It's better to buy them on sale.

When shopping for clothes, on the other hand, it's often a good idea not to plan too far ahead. In the late summer and fall, winter clothes are at a premium. By January, they're all on sale.

And it's perfectly acceptable for everyone in the family—young people, parents, grandparents alike—to keep a list of needed practical gifts. This is true at all times, but especially true for the new graduate, who may well need a half-dozen white shirts a lot more than he needs the monogrammed blazer from a grandparent who's not quite sure what's appropriate.

Finally, here's the most important shopping tip: No impulse buying. Shop from a list. This is true when you go out to a store, and it's equally true when you surf the Internet, with all those one-click opportunities to buy.

The Big Buying Issue: A Car

Because this is the first really big expense a teenager is likely to incur, and because so much is riding on the decision, let's go over all the buying decisions again as they relate to this special case.

The Brand

Choosing to buy a brand name or a generic isn't an issue with cars—they're all brand names. But there are huge differences in price, and huge differences in value. There are many, many sources for information on value and reliability of different brands—general consumer magazines and specialized auto magazines, like *Car and Driver.* But before you start narrowing down the field by brand and price, you and your teen need to discuss what she needs in a car.

The number one issue here is SAFETY.

If your teen doesn't think it's the number one issue, then your teen is wrong. Your vote on this matter, however, is the only one that counts, and this is true whether you're helping to pay for the car or not. A car is too important—a safe car is too important—for you not to have veto power over the decision.

This brings up another issue specific to car buying: the money issue. I've said over and over again in this book and in all the workshops I've given that it's your responsibility to pay for the basics and that your teen has to pay for any extras she wants, like a fancy brand name.

The reverse is true in car buying.

If your teen can only afford so much for a car, and that amount won't buy the right amount of safety (nonnegotiable and determined by you), then I recommend that you pay whatever it takes to make up the difference and put her in a car that you'll feel good about her driving.

This only seems like a contradiction in terms. It's not. The difference between a pair of sneakers and a pair of Yohji Yamamoto trainers is a difference in frills. The difference between a car without antilock brakes or up-to-date air bags and a car you can trust is a difference in essentials.

Here's a list of important safety features.

- **Antilock brakes.** These help to prevent skidding out of control when you have to slam on the brakes suddenly. There's some debate over the effectiveness of antilock brakes. Most safety experts agree that they work well if used properly, *but they can actually be dangerous if you use them wrong.* Make sure your teen asks the dealer to explain the proper way to use them, do a demonstration, and have your teen practice using them in a test drive.

- **Daytime running lights.** This is a relatively new concept, but they're now required on cars in Canada and several European countries. They're like high-beam headlights, but with a greatly reduced intensity, and they make a car more visible to oncoming drivers. They can help prevent two-car crashes.

- **Air bags.** When they're used properly, they can save lives (20 percent fewer deaths in head-on collisions with air bags, 15 percent fewer in all crashes). "Used properly" means always wear a seat belt, and make sure children under age 13 sit in the backseat.

- **Side-impact protection.** An important new safety feature is the inclusion of side guard beams and side padding, which can protect a driver in the event of a potentially deadly side-impact collision. Some new cars are even being equipped with side air bags. Look into all these features.

- **Head restraints.** These are standard on all new cars. Some people don't like them, but they're important in preventing a driver's (or passenger's) head from snapping back in a rear-end crash. Make sure your teen driver keeps the head restraint high enough so that it rests directly behind the back of his head.

- **The right tires.** Tires are no area to cut corners. They're the only part of your car that actually keeps it on the road. Make sure that your tires have enough tread on them to be safe.

Let Abe and George Help

How good are your tires? Try this coin test.

Place a penny, with the back of the coin upside down, into several tread grooves across the tire. If the top of the Lincoln Memorial is always covered by the tread, you have more than $6/32$ inch of tread depth remaining, and you're in good shape. But if you're going to be driving on snow and ice, you should start thinking about new tires when you get below $6/32$ inch.

Now place a quarter, with the front of the coin upside down, into several tread grooves across the tire. If part of Washington's head is always covered by the tread, you have more than $4/32$ inch of tread depth remaining. You need at least $4/32$ inch to feel secure about driving in heavy rain. So if you can see all of George, and you live in a rainy area, it's time to shop for new tires.

Now try the penny again, with the front of the coin upside down. If you can see all of Lincoln's head, you have $2/32$ inch of tread depth or less remaining, and you're driving on dangerous tires. Less than $2/32$ inch, and your tires are illegal in most states.

- **Four-wheel drive.** This can be useful if you live in a part of the country that has bad weather and slick roads. You don't, however, want your teenager thinking that it's an off-road vehicle for horsing around in. The best thing to do about bad weather is not drive in it. And don't consider buying your teen, or letting your teen buy, an SUV.

- **A cell phone.** Don't let your teenager leave home without it. And make sure he knows that *you don't talk on it while driving.* There's more and more evidence to show that this is a significant distraction, and a significant contributor to accidents.

• **Directional aids.** A service like OnStar is terrific, but it's still a luxury item. At the very least, make sure that your teenager has a really good atlas and state and local maps in her car.

These are the extras you should consider paying for. Some of them are standard with new or newer cars, which means you may want to make up the difference between an older used car that doesn't have them all and a newer car that does. Other extras, like a CD player and state-of-the-art speakers, are your child's responsibility.

An Unmarked Police Car

One reason for carrying a cell phone—and an important piece of advice for any young driver, especially a young female driver:

Never stop if you're signaled to pull over by an unmarked police car on a deserted stretch of highway.

Anyone can put a flashing blue light on the top of his car, and there is no way of knowing if it's really a police car. And this is, unfortunately, a common technique used by rapists.

If you're signaled by a police car's flashing lights on a deserted stretch of road—even if it's a marked car—don't stop. Put your flashers on and continue driving slowly to a safe place, such as a gas station or a convenience store parking lot. A real police officer won't expect you to stop in a dangerous place.

Use your cell phone to call 911, and explain the situation to them, so that they can call the officers in the car that's following you, and advise them of your plans.

Or—if the car following you is a fake—they can stop that car and arrest the driver.

New or Used?

New cars come equipped with the newest safety features, but so do late-model used cars—a car that's only a year or two old. And the used car is going to be a lot cheaper. This means you may even be able to afford a closer-to-top-of-the-line car, with better engineering and better safety features.

If you're considering a used car, make sure that it's a good one. This generally means getting it from a dealer who'll give you a good warranty.

Also, look for signs that the car has been ill-treated. And remember, cars aren't like puppies. You can't take one that's been mistreated and nurse it back to health. Serious damage to a car is likely to leave you with serious, long-term problems. It may also be wise to go online get a Carfax vehicle history report, which will give you important information like whether the car has ever been in an accident, how many owners it had, and whether it was ever recalled by the manufacturer for repair work. You can find the service at www.carfax.com.

Here are some things to check out on a used car.

- **Body.** Does it show signs of having been in a collision? Are the seams straight? Are all the panels the same color? Are there ripples and dents in the surface? Do the doors close cleanly?

- **Frame.** Have the car lifted up so you can look under it. Are there any places that look crumpled and straightened? You can sometimes find evidence of body damage in the trunk, in the wheel wells, or under the hood, too.

- **Leaks.** Anything dripping under the car? What color is it? Any stains where it has been parked?

- **Tires.** Do more than kick the tires. Are they all the same brand? The same size? Do they show even wear and tear? Also, does the car come equipped with a good spare, a jack, and a lug wrench?

- **Interior.** Stains and bad smells are a bad sign. You may not want to buy a car from a heavy smoker, since that smell doesn't go away quickly, and it can't be doing your health much good. Mildew and dampness can indicate serious problems.

  Do the windows go up and down easily? Do the seats adjust smoothly? Do all the seat belts look in perfect shape? Do they open and close easily? Have the air bags ever been activated?

- **Suspension.** First, make sure the vehicle looks level to the ground. Then bounce each corner. They should all bounce back one or two times, and there should be no creaking noise when bouncing.

- **Lights.** Make a complete tour of the lights. Headlights, brights, both front and back turn signals, brake lights—make sure every one of them is working.

Buy or Lease?

Teens often don't even consider leasing a car—maybe because it seems like a sort of middle-aged thing to do, maybe because if it's the teenager's first car, he wants the thrill of owning it.

But actually, leasing can make a lot of sense. The variables that can make leasing so attractive are cost, warranty, and long-term considerations.

To help understand the difference in costs, consider the information in "Leasing: Cost Analysis."

The mileage limit is an interesting factor, in terms of the teenage driver. It means you're putting a certain amount of pressure on your teen not to drive too much, which may be something that sounds like a bad idea to him, but a good idea to you.

You and your teen need to have a serious conversation here. How much does your teen legitimately need to be driving? If this is

LEASING: COST ANALYSIS

Pros	Cons	What You Need to Ask
Basically, it costs less, which means you can either spend less than you'd budgeted for, or spend the same amount and get a better car. It's something to think about when both budget and safety are important considerations. Your down payment—yes, there's a down payment with leasing—is likely to be lower, and your monthly payments are less, which may bring them down to within your teenager's budget. You pay sales tax only on the portion of the car you finance, so that's another saving.	It might not cost less. For one thing, lease contracts are confusing, so you can't always be sure you're getting a fair deal. For another, leased cars have mileage limits—if you drive over the limit, you're going to be paying per mile.	Exactly what the deal is. Get them to put all the numbers in writing, including what the car will be worth at the end of the rental period. How much do you really drive? If it's going to be over the limit, how much? How much is the per-mile charge? You may still be ahead of the deal even after you pay it. Consider this: You may be able to negotiate a higher mileage limit.

a first car, you may well want him to ease into it slowly and not drive huge amounts until he gets some experience under his belt. And don't forget, driving less—like not driving back and forth to school every day—can mean lower insurance rates. You can put a curfew on driving, too. In some states, young drivers aren't permitted to drive after dark. You can institute your own rules, too, for slightly older teen drivers—no driving after 11:00 P.M., for example.

Whether the warranty provisions of a lease work in your favor depends on how you expect your teen to treat the car. Make sure she understands the cost of careless driving, and make sure she knows that she'll bear that cost. (For more information, see "Leasing: Repairs.")

It also pays to look ahead to what your situation may be at the end of the lease. As you make your decision, take a look at "Leasing: Long-Term View" on page 292.

In general, buy a car if:

- You plan to keep it for longer than the time you'd be paying for it.

- You know you'll be putting a lot of mileage on the car.

- You can actually get a better deal buying than leasing. (This may be possible if a dealer is offering zero percent financing.)

In general, lease a car if:

- You can get a better deal leasing than buying (see "The Deal" on page 293).

Bottom line, if you're considering leasing a car, you need to know four things.

What will it cost me during the term of the lease? Remember that the higher the residual value, the lower the monthly fee. But if you think you may want to buy the car at the end of the lease, then a high residual fee is a bad idea. Remember that capitalized cost is simply the sticker price of the car, and it may be negotiable. Also, ask about gap insurance, which covers the difference between what the car is worth and what you currently owe, in the case of theft or a serious accident.

LEASING: REPAIRS

Pros	Cons	What You Need to Ask
With a 3-year lease, the factory warranty covers most repairs, so if you keep the car only for the length of the lease, your repair costs can be a lot less than they'd be with a car you buy and keep longer. This is, by the way, the reason a 36-month lease is your best bet.	When you turn it in, you're going to be paying for a lot of dings and scrapes that you'd never think twice about on a car you owned. And it can be even worse than you think. I was charged $350 for losing the owner's manual on a leased car that I turned in.	Find out what will be considered excessive wear and tear and how the cost of damages is figured.

What will it cost me up front? Typically, the front-end costs include sales tax, security, and the first month's lease payment. Make sure that the sales tax only covers what you're actually paying for—the capitalized cost minus the residual fee. Sometimes a company may waive the security deposit.

What might it cost me at the end of the lease? Make sure you know how they define reasonable wear and tear. If you're concerned about mileage, see if the dealer will extend the mileage limits. Also, if the cost per mile is not too high, you may still end up paying less for leasing than for buying. Make sure you understand the penalty for early termination.

Who am I actually leasing from? If you're considering leasing a car from a specific dealership or leasing company, you need to know if the leasing company is the vehicle's manufacturing company. If it's not, a warning flag should go up. If it's not, and they're offering you a deal that seems too good to be true, a second flag

LEASING: LONG-TERM VIEW

Pros	Cons	What You Need to Ask
You don't have trade-in hassles at the end of the lease.	You don't have a car at the end of the lease unless you decide to buy it at that point.	What's the residual value of the car going to be? What will I have to pay if I want to buy it?
You're stuck with the car for only 3 years.	You *are* stuck with the car for 3 years, and it's very hard to break a lease.	Will your teenager's life circumstances change a lot over the next 3 years? If a lease is a good idea now, are there reasons why it might not be 2 years from now?
You can keep driving a new or nearly new car for a reasonable monthly payment.	Your monthly payment never ends. You'll never be driving a slightly older car that you aren't sending someone a check for each month.	How important is a new car? If your teen is a careful driver, and mechanically handy, and wants a car that she'll keep for a long time, a lease may not be such a good idea.

should go up. If they're offering you a deal that seems too good to be true, and the explanation of the deal is complicated and hard to follow, you should be out the door.

Online or Brick and Mortar?

The Internet has changed the whole experience of car buying, mostly for the better. Car salesmen, over the years, have developed

The Deal

So how do you figure out how much a leasing deal going to cost you?

There are three main variables that you need to consider (and if the dealer starts throwing a lot more variables at you, it may be time to scratch that dealer off your list).

1. Price. In leasing a car, as in buying, there's a price tag. Even though you're not buying the car, someone is—the leasing company. And as with a car you buy, the price is negotiable. So start by negotiating that. The lower the capitalized cost (that's what they call it in lease-speak), the lower the lease.

2. Residual value. This number is what they predict the car will be worth at the end of the lease—generally a little more than half the sticker price after 3 years. But the residual value can be tinkered with, too. If the dealer figures it as higher, your monthly payments can be lower. This is a really bad idea if you plan to buy the car at the end of the lease. If you don't, it can save you a few bucks.

(*A note here:* If you lease a car with a high residual value, make sure you know in advance that you're not going to buy it at the end of the lease, and don't let a salesperson talk you into changing your mind, because they'll try.)

3. Interest rate. Actually, in lease language, car dealers really don't talk about interest rate, they talk about money factor. It's the same thing, only different numbers. They have the pocket calculators in front of them, so have them convert it back and tell you what the interest rate is.

Gap Insurance

Gap insurance covers the gap between what an insurance company will pay in the case of theft or accident, and what the leasing company says the car is worth.

The son of a friend of mine had his leased car stolen. The insurance company valued it at several thousand dollars less than the figure he was still required to pay the leasing company, and now he's stuck with that debt.

You don't have to get gap insurance, but I recommend it strongly—especially if you're leasing a high-end car. The importance of this particular insurance rises in proportion to the value of the car, for two reasons: The gap in dollars will be greater with a high-end car, and high-end cars are more likely to be stolen.

Shop around for gap insurance. Rates can be widely different. If you decide to get it, remember that this becomes part of the cost of leasing.

a stereotyped reputation for sleaziness, and while that's certainly unfair as a generalization, it's not based on nothing either. Traditionally, buying a car was a complicated transaction filled with so many variables and so much fine print that it could be very hard to figure out exactly what you were paying and exactly what you were getting for it. Most car-lot salesmen will avoid quoting you a price at all until they're sure you're hooked on the car.

With Internet sites like Edmunds, J. D. Power and Associates, and Kelley Blue Book, it's easy to find out what a car is really worth, and use that information to come up with a price you're willing to pay.

The principal advantage to buying a car over the Internet is price. According to researchers at J. D. Power, the typical Internet buyer saves $500 over a buyer of the same car from a dealership.

You can shop over the Internet using the Internet department of a conventional dealership, or you can use a site like CarsDirect.com, which will search nationwide for the specific car you want, so that even if your nearby dealer doesn't have one in stock that matches the color you want and the number of cup holders you need, you still have a shot at finding one someplace.

The principal disadvantage? Well, if you're in Omaha and buying a Toyota Corolla from a dealer in Raleigh, you're not going to be test-driving it. And while you can get a certain amount of information—actually, a lot of information—from the Internet, you may prefer to have a live human being answering your specific questions.

An alternative that may perhaps combine the best of both worlds? Shop the Internet, get a price, go and present it to your local dealer, and ask him to match it.

When to Buy

It's pretty much a myth that there's one better time of the year—or the week or the month—to buy a new car. New models used to be introduced in the fall, meaning that there was more pressure on the dealers to get rid of the old cars on the lot, but that's no longer the case. New models may be introduced earlier rather than later in the year, and whatever time you buy, there are still going to be figures the dealer would like you to pay, and bottom-line figures. There's no substitute for going in armed with knowledge, and no substitute for shopping around.

20

KIDS MOVING BACK HOME

Your financial involvement with your kids' lives doesn't always end when they leave home, or even when they leave college.

You'll have housewarming gifts for them when they get their first apartment, and christening gifts and college funds for your grandchildren. Oh, yes, and little things like weddings. How much you choose to pay for a wedding, how much—if at all—you want your child to chip in, that's up to you, just as how much you want to spend for a graduation present is up to you.

Part of your decision making will surround the entire question of parental generosity. That's really a personal issue for you to decide. But regardless of how generous you want to be, you want your adult child to become a responsible financial citizen of the household, the community, the country, the world.

That responsibility doesn't develop all at once or on the same schedule for everyone. So what happens if your grown child has to move back home for economic reasons?

You need rules.

They can't be the same rules that you used when your kids were minors and you were completely responsible for them. Neither can they be like the roommate contracts I discussed in chapter 16. Your kids aren't your roommates, and it's still your house.

You need some combination of the two, with some unique wrinkles thrown in for good measure.

Sometimes Good Chickens Come Home to Roost

All kinds of blended families exist, and one of the more common ones in recent years has become adult children/older parents. Sometimes this means children in their twenties or thirties, with young kids of their own, getting help with finances and child care. Sometimes it means middle-aged children taking care of elderly parents in varying stages of health.

Studies indicate that it sounds like more of a burden than it actually is—that in fact both elder parents and grown children say they like the arrangement and wouldn't want to change it.

It takes some getting used to, like any other arrangement between people. Roberta Maisel, a sociologist, mediator, and author of *All Grown Up: Living Happily Ever After with Your Adult Children*, urges the conscious creation of "a new family paradigm, one that's close to equality but still recognizes the parents' valuable life experiences."

There are two issues you must deal with, and you need to make sure that both of these are clarified right from the start. The first is "who pays for what," and the second is "my house, my rules."

And both of these are dependent on a couple of other key variables: Is this a long- or short-term plan? And are there grand-children involved?

Who Pays for What?

Is your grown child moving back in because she's temporarily hard up and needs some financial help to get back on her feet? It can happen, and it doesn't mean she's been irresponsible, dumb, or lazy. Circumstances change suddenly in the best-planned of lives. Most commonly, a young mother or father who's primarily been staying home taking care of the kids can suddenly suffer the loss of a partner. Or a business venture can collapse, even if it's been planned well.

Or maybe it was planned poorly. Or maybe your child just made mistakes. Those things can happen, too, and you're not going to just throw her to the wolves.

If it's a case of financial hardship, you'll want to adjust the financial arrangement accordingly. Your goal should be to make it easy enough on her that she'll be able to save up enough (or pay enough of her debts) to start over, but without giving her a free ride. You also need to take your own financial needs and abilities into account. Don't extend yourself more than you can.

In other words, make a plan while considering the following two questions.

How much does your child need? Your goal is to help her get on her feet so that she can start out again with a solid chance of success. The two of you need to come up with a dollar figure that will give her that. You'll need two figures:

- Amount needed to get out of debt _____

- Amount in savings to provide a cushion _____

How much can your child expect to earn by herself? These figures aren't written in stone, and you can adjust them as time goes on to reflect actual conditions. But if she's working part-time as a clerk at Toys "R" Us while she finishes a degree in electrical engineering, you have one set of expectations. And if she's on strike and working full-time at the local convenience store while waiting for a new, painfully fought out labor agreement, you have another. If she wants to move back home for 6 months to work full-time on finishing her novel, that's yet a different set of circumstances. So figure:

- Earning now _____

- Expected earning in 6 months _____

- Expected earning in a year _____

This gives you something to go on. How much does your child need to lay aside? How much can she afford to contribute to that fund each month? How much does that leave for her to contribute to household expenses? Can you afford to cover the rest?

These are all subject to negotiation. The more she's able to put aside, the sooner she'll be able to move out—but the more you'll have to contribute. Figure out what works for both of you.

Loan or Gift?

Do you expect to be paid back for your contribution to getting your grown child back on his feet? That's up to you. I think it's a good idea to consider the help that you're giving over this period as a loan, but that's a personal decision.

Tax Consequences?

Check with a tax expert, but you may be able to claim your child as a dependent if he makes less than $2,750 for the year and you provide over half of his support. If he is under the age of 24 and meets the definition of a full-time student, you can claim him regardless of his income. Single parents with single adult children who have lived at home for at least half a year also might save taxes by filing as a head of household.

—Financial Planning Association

If you are considering it a loan, decide how much interest you'll charge (or if you'll charge interest—again, this is up to you, but I always believe it's a good idea to remember that money and time both have value), and calculate a loan repayment schedule into your plan.

Long-Term Arrangement

If you've decided to live as an extended family because you all like the idea—you're close and you believe it's the best way to live—then living expenses should be apportioned in whatever ratio they're incurred.

Sign of the Times

According to the most recent census, the number of households with three generations under one roof has doubled in the past 20 years, while the number of young adults moving back home is up 6 percent—80 million families have a grown child living at home.

And you might want to consider figuring out an arrangement in which your child buys some equity in your house.

Whose House, Whose Rules?

If your offspring is moving back in temporarily, you need to make it clear just what the rules are. They probably can't be the same as they were when he lived at home before, but then, rules for our kids are always changing. At a certain age, there's no more nap time. At another age, they don't have to be home for dinner every night. Curfews get extended.

So how do you want things to be at this stage in your child's life? It still is your house, and your rules, and they can be anything you want them to be.

A curfew? I suppose you could. I don't recommend it for, say, a 22-year-old. But calling in to let you know he won't be home when you were expecting him? That doesn't seem unreasonable. You never stop worrying about your kids' safety.

For me, there will never be an age when calling in isn't a non-negotiable demand. I go nuts if I expect my kids to be home and I don't know where they are.

Not long ago, I found out, to my surprise, that it's a non-negotiable demand for them, too. I went out to a party with friends and found to my surprise that I was having such a great time that I stayed way, way late, after which a small but fun-filled group of us repaired to an all-night diner for scrambled eggs, coffee, and more conversation. When I got in at 4:00 A.M., I found both of my teenage kids waiting up for me with stern expressions on their faces. And they weren't kidding.

The next day, they called a family meeting to discuss it, and I was on the carpet.

It almost sounds like a joke—that they were playing a role-reversal game on me. But it wasn't.

"Don't ever stay out like that without calling us," they said. "What were you thinking?"

I found myself saying the same thing my kids have said to me—and every kid has said to her parents after breaking curfew.

"I was having a good time," I said. "I knew I was all right."

"And that's supposed to make us feel better? Anything could have happened to you."

"I don't see why you're making such a big deal about this."

"We bet you don't. You didn't even have your cell phone turned on."

"I wouldn't have heard it anyway—the music was too loud."

"And that's an excuse? You are never to do this again. If you're going to be out late, call and let us know. That's nonnegotiable."

Having guests of the opposite sex stay over? Only if you're comfortable with it. Not if you aren't. It's your house, and it's not a God-given right. For that matter, you need to decide about guests in general, and certainly about parties.

Smoking? Not if you don't allow it in the house, not even in your grown child's own room.

Who buys food? Who pays for it? Whose food is whose? This can be a fertile area for problems. There may be no one, of any age, who doesn't feel that it's okay to go into Mom's refrigerator and help himself to whatever's there. If that's not okay with you, make sure your new boarder knows what the rules are.

More problematic is the grandchild question. You really need to make sure this one is understood on both sides.

Are some rooms off-limits to little ones? You have every right to make this rule. But since little ones don't always understand those rules, installing locks on those doors may be a good idea.

Are you going to help out with child care? How much? You may want to make an exact schedule. Or you may want to institute a rule that says you need 24 hours' notification if you're going to be asked to babysit. Or perhaps a maximum-hours-per-week rule.

What is your discipline and parenting style versus your child's style? Better to talk about that in advance than in the heat of some kind of dispute.

What are your limits? Even if you don't want to make any specific limitations in advance, and you can't see how you could possibly ever have too much of your adorable grandkids, you still *must* make this understood: You can say no, if it's inconvenient for you. It cannot be taken for granted that you take care of the kids. And if you're having a party, and you don't want kids there, you're allowed to say that little Frankie needs to go stay with a friend or a sitter for the evening.

Setting rules is the key to a successful "crowded nest." If you suddenly spring them on your child without warning, however, it can cause hard feelings. These things need to be discussed explicitly in advance, especially regarding their children.

Rules are important if the move home is temporary, and they are mandatory if the move home is long-term. These are potential minefields. I wouldn't begin to presume to give advice about how to work out every single one of them—just that you have to work them out, or they'll explode on you.

If There Are Serious Problems

In case of serious illness—physical or mental—all these rules take a backseat to the immediate crisis, and these are problems outside the scope of this book. But here's a note on dealing with an adult addict who moves back home.

MARIA

"I HAD GIVEN UP HOPE."

Maria is a retired Army nurse living in Florida. She has three children; her addicted son was the youngest.

"It is difficult to *not* allow your adult child back in the house if he or she is going to be homeless. It takes a lot to finally stop enabling and say, 'This is it.' We set up contracts, often written: no drug usage; no drug-addicted friends in the house; get a job; take over some of the chores; keep your room clean; if you are not going to be home for a meal, notify us. Go to your 12-step program . . . 90 meetings in 90 days, contact your sponsor. When we got snappy remarks about his age and 'all these rules,' we reminded him it was our home, and he either followed the rules or found somewhere else to live. He hated being home by midnight. I finally packed his suitcase and left it on the front porch.

"The verbal abuse is difficult when you are used to a loving atmosphere where people rarely raise their voices and there are warm exchanges as a rule. It is hard to have your addict in the house, but often more difficult after you lock your door to him. It was more than 2 years before we saw signs that maybe he would be clean!

"Now we get a call several times during the week; he shares his life with us, and especially our granddaughter. Sometimes too much, but I wouldn't even consider suggesting he not call so much. Our daughter-in-law says that she thinks it is wonderful we have so much to talk about. . . . Her family was never like that.

"I thank God daily that our son is part of our lives and that he has made such positive changes in his life. I had given up hope!"

21

WRAPPING IT UP

Well, there's no getting around it. I'm an organization freak. I believe in having checklists, using No-Magic-Money Logs, and writing down the pros and cons before making a major purchase. I underline passages and write notes in the margins of books, and I put self-stick notes everywhere. When my kids were young, I had chore lists for them on the refrigerator. I do everything except use an electronic organizer, because I don't quite trust anything that can go *poof!* and lose everything all of a sudden.

So what better way to sum up this book than a checklist? Here are some of the main points I've made. Take a look at them and see how they apply to you.

(continued on page 308)

Action Item	I Do This	I'm Going to Start Doing This	This Just Isn't Me/ Doesn't Apply
I don't let nagging or wheedling affect my decision if I don't think it's appropriate to give my teens money for something.			
I've bitten my tongue, stopped myself from saying, "We can't afford it," and instead said, "This doesn't fit into our budget."			
I don't fork over money to my teens without knowing what it's for.			
I've kept a No-Magic-Money Log to account for my spending.			
I have a good idea of what my teens spend their money on.			
I've gotten my teens to keep a No-Magic-Money Log to account for their spending.			
I have a good idea of where my teens get their money.			
My teens have a realistic idea of our family's income bracket.			
My teens have a realistic idea of our family's savings.			
I involve my teenagers in family budget planning.			
I involve my teenagers in family bill paying.			
I've talked to my teens about advertising hype and peer pressure.			
I know that my teens understand the basics of tipping and the reason for tipping.			
I've made sure my teens understand that a credit card is a loan, with a very specific re-payment contract.			
I've made sure my teens understand how credit card interest works, and how much "paying the minimum" can cost them.			
I know how many credit cards my teens have and what they are.			

Action Item	I Do This	I'm Going to Start Doing This	This Just Isn't Me/ Doesn't Apply
I know how much credit card debt my teens have.			
My teens know that they're responsible for paying their own auto insurance or the additional costs to my premiums.			
My teens know what to do in case they're involved in an auto accident. I know that they know because they've told me, step by step.			
My teens and I have discussed how much they should be working and how much time they need to devote to school.			
I've visited my teens' workplaces.			
My teens understand what fixed and variable expenses are.			
For me, buying kids' clothes means buying the basics, not the expensive brand names.			
My teens are involved in preparing for the expense of their college education.			
My teens have opened their own checking accounts.			
I've made sure my teens have a contract on expenses with roommates.			
I've put my teens on some form of "starter" credit card.			
My teens understand the importance of paying off credit card debt.			
My teens know how to get their credit histories.			
I've discussed résumé writing with my teens.			
I've discussed "smart shopping" with my teens.			
My teens always carry cell phones while driving (and know not to use them while driving).			

If you have a lot of check marks in the second column, start making a timetable to move them over to the first column. If you have a lot in the third column . . . ultimately, these are all your decisions. You know best what works for you. Still, take a look at that list again. Why is this point or that point "just not you"? Because it's wrong for you—or because you don't think you can do it?

If it's wrong for you, you really do know best. It's your life, and no self-help book can ever take the place of your best judgment.

If you think you can't, that's another story. Think again. You can do anything.

ACKNOWLEDGMENTS

I'd like to thank my agent, Peter Ginsberg, for his talent, insights, and patience. Eric Martins, my lawyer, thanks for the "legalling." Ed Dratch, I love the numbers. Ron Ries, thanks for being there. Claudette, for your wisdom, feng shui, and love—I don't want to do it without you. Tad, thanks for your voice, your soul, and for "Packwood." Bill, thanks for being serious and kind . . . words can't describe. Dr. Valerie Spangenberg, thanks for keeping my wings on straight. Mitchell Waters, friend, confidant, and the keeper of the commas: thanks. Suzelle, and you thought things were good now—I'll show you how good it will be. To Shmuli, thank you for connecting us to what's really important. For Chani, I can't think of a better role model for our daughters. My kids, my heart—Alison, always there to reglue my tail or whatever other body part needs gluing. Irv, your brilliance to change the world. Trevor, Whitney, David, Crystal, Ryan, Laura, Anthony, and Charles, my children that I have wrinkles from but not stretch marks. For research, advice, and information in putting this book together, there are so many, but let me at least mention Donna Jackson, Patti Marshock, Laura Marshock, and Jody Jessen.

Also thank you to the good people at Rodale who helped bring clarity to my message through editing and design, including Lou Cinquino, Karen Neely, Trish Field, Keith Biery, Donna Bellis, and Tara Long.

INDEX

T

U

ABOUT THE AUTHORS

Neale S. Godfrey is the chairman of the Children's Financial Network, the founder of the First Children's Bank, and the former president of the First Women's Bank. She has sold nearly 1 million copies of her previous books, including two *New York Times* bestsellers, *Money Doesn't Grow on Trees* and *A Penny Saved*. Her frequent television appearances include *Oprah, Good Morning America, Today,* and CNBC. She has trained thousands of teenagers and young adults in financial responsibility, including her own son and daughter.

Tad Richards has collaborated with Neale Godfrey on other family finance books, including *A Penny Saved*. He is the author of *My Night with the Language Thieves,* a collection of poetry, and *Situations,* a novel in verse.